Seriously Cancer...Seriously?

Seriously Cancer...Seriously?

When his cancer returned, we chose to LIVE

CHRISTY L LEONARD

To all of the amazing friends and family who supported us during our journey. To my friends who inspired me to keep writing. To Nikki, who never gave up on me. To my parents who taught me to make lemonade out of lemons. To my five boys, you are his legacy, keep being amazing. Thank you for pushing me to keep going…to keep living. Thank you for being the loves of my life.

To Tony…The sun came up today, I chose to **LIVE**!!!

Table of contents

Preface

What you are about to read is the raw story of a death as it unfolded in real time, and how it impacted multiple lives. It is just one more battle story in the ongoing war against cancer – a diary of a thousand small defeats and even more victories – some past, and some that will hopefully come in the future.

This is also a very, very human story told in a very, very, human way by a woman who found strength she never thought she had, and learned that sometimes, in the end, strength alone is not enough. It is Tony Leonard's story, a story of the Iraq war contractor, father, husband, brother, son, and friend's fight against the odds, time, and his own body.

Through these pages you will meet Tony, a man who, after fighting nearly the better part of a decade, lost his battle with cancer on January 22, 2019. Tony's life became a continuous, ferocious, battle against an intractable and cunning enemy, but he never let that enemy define who or what he was or how he chose to live whatever time was allotted to him.

It is also a story about caregiving and sacrifice. That story belongs to Tony's wife Christy Leonard, and their sons. But Christy is no more a victim than Tony. In taking care of her husband and children she found something inside herself, something that had always been there but was only summoned when it is needed. Christy is not some shy, faceless heroine standing by her man. She is also a warrior, fighting her own battles and she fights his.

In a sense, Tony's story is also all of our stories, since it causes us to ask ourselves if we are living as full a life as he did when he discovered he would never grow old.

What makes his story all the more compelling is that it is not the story of extraordinary people, but rather the unique record of quite ordinary people facing, and rising above, extraordinary challenges.

Without cancer, unless you lived in Fayetteville, NC you might have gone your entire life without ever having heard of Tony Leonard. Without cancer, Tony would have enjoyed a long life with his great loves, Christy and his sons Anthoney, Alec, Austin, Aydin, and Ashton.

Without cancer, there would have been a lifetime of predictable fights over the small, ordinary things families squabble about, and celebrations of the things that may seem small to some, but, in the end, mean everything – birthdays, school sporting events, cell phones at the table, first loves, proms, the joys and pains of growing old together as a family, and watching as new generations take their place at holiday dinner tables.

But there was cancer, and that changed everything. What you are about to read are a series of remarkable dispatches from a long journey in pursuit of, "freedom froms"– freedom from disease, freedom from pain, and freedom from loss. It is also a diary of, "freedom tos" – freedom to hope, freedom to dream, freedom to love, and freedom to accept.

The author, Christy L Leonard (Murphy), hasn't given us fully a fully polished story, all nice and completely linear and logical. Instead, she is giving us a sequential peek into what it is like to battle a disease, the medical establishment, the United States Congress, and – perhaps most importantly – your own fear.

Spoiler Alert: This isn't the story of a miraculous cure or divine intervention. It is a comeback story of a sort, but – on one level at least – it doesn't have a happy ending. The hero dies, as we quickly realize he must. But his death and the steps toward that death are a source of inspiration.

In these pages you'll meet a man who refused to let death cheat him out of the life he wanted to live or the love of his wife and children. Tony died all right, but only after he lived with more passion and more commitment than most of us will ever know.

And, as you read, you'll get to know Christy, a still young woman who thought the pain and turmoil of her earlier years had finally brought her to a place of peace she could occupy for the rest of her life. Her marriage to Tony provided a sense of permanence, stability, and unconditional love that did, in fact, live a lifetime, just one that was sadly all too brief.

You'll also meet Tony and Christy's family, the parents that supported them, and the young boys called on to become young men too soon. And you will learn the lengths that their mother went to shield them as much as she could from the pain of the reality they shared. You will read about how Tony, after 19 days in the hospital somehow summoned the strength to make it to one of Aydin's football games, and how he created time to work through his own, "bucket list," realizing each checkmark robbed him of some of his once formidable strength and time, a dying person's most valuable asset.

You will also realize how Tony and Christy's sacrifices and pain helped, and continue to help, the plight of all those with stomach cancers. Note I didn't say cancer victims, because there aren't any victims in these pages. No, this is a record of champions and winners who fought and won the toughest battle of them all – not cancer – but keeping faith with themselves and each other in the face of odds they came to know were unbeatable.

There are lessons in this book for all of us about how to live, how to love, how to battle, and how to preserve grace in defeat.

If this were a novel we might find the characters incompletely drawn. We would complain that the author showed them in contradictory lights: selfish at some point, selfless at others; by turns objective and hyper-rational and then furiously emotional; calculated and precise at times and totally spontaneous at others. But, there are also what writers call, "through lines," as well: love, passion, courage, and the ability to stare down fears most of us hope only to know in nightmares.

The reason these characters refuse to, "stay in character," is that they aren't products of a novelist's imagination. These are real, authentic, human beings just like you or me. The only difference? Most of us lack the courage Tony, Christy, and their children were forced to summon each and every moment of each and every day.

Sure, what you are about to read may seem fragmentary in points, possible even contradictory at others but, if that's how you read it then you have forgotten what you are reading; selections of an ongoing blog Christy kept adding to throughout the course of Tony's battle with cancer. Life is messy, and the most organized of lines are neither scripted nor predictable.

Christy wasn't trying to be clever, or polished, or witty, or inspirational, or impress us. She was trying to tell all those who loved, and came to love, her and her family what she felt in the moment. It is an amazing testament not just to the Leonard family, but to families everywhere facing shared challenges and setbacks.

Tony's Facebook page is still active, because Tony's story continues on without him. At the top of that page is a quote from him that sums up his warrior spirit. "Living strong and loving life," it reads, "six years and the fight drives on... kiss my booty cancer." Tony wasn't some macho Alpha male challenging Death. He had seen enough real death in the Middle East to fall for the temptation to find comfort in false bravado.

Toward the end of his life Tony came to understand what all combat soldiers know: to go into battle is to risk death and, while you may not have any choice about the hand you are dealt, you always have a choice about how you play it. By any account, he played it with courage and like a champion, doing everything he could to secure the ground so that the next wave of troops in the battle against cancer would be in a better and safer position.

So, remember if there is occasional rage where you were expecting tears here it is because this is the story of several lives, well lived and hearts and spirits that could be bent but never broken.

And, when you have finished, put down this book and ask yourself if you think you have the courage of a Tony, or a Christy, or of their children. If you found yourself in a shell crater on some foreign battlefield with death relentlessly charging you would you leap to your feet to engage it on your terms, or would you try to bury yourself deeper in the false shelter of that crater?

Let's hope you never have to face that day. Here is the unvarnished, plainspoken story of a family that did.

Hey Doc... I Think I Have an Ulcer

November 5, 2011

Its Nov 5, Tony turns 39 and it's time for our yearly physicals.

"Hey Doc, be sure to ask Tony about his stomach," I say. "It's been bothering him a lot lately when he eats. He's stubborn and won't tell you." Little did I know how that simple request would change our lives forever.

A month later, its time to meet with the GI doc to schedule his endoscopy (scope). Because of the holidays, we get in on January 26, 2012.

"No ulcer, no hernia, no tumors. Everything looks great! Just some irritation but it's probably just some bacteria; the biopsies will tell us for sure," says the doc, as Tony and I high five each other.

A few days later, we get a letter that he has a follow up in a month. Double high fives.

Friday 2/3/12 8:30am - RING, RING....Who is calling me this early? "Yes ma'am this is the nurse from the doctor's office. We need your husband to come in tomorrow morning at 0800 if at all possible."

"I'm sorry. What did you say," I ask. "On a Saturday? Who wants to see their patient on a Saturday?" I drop the phone and broke down.

After losing my brother to lung cancer almost two years before to the day, I knew what that phone call was all about.

Now I had to tell Tony without him worrying...

The News

February 2, 2012

"What do I wear?" I thought. "Do I wear makeup? Does it matter? It will just run everywhere." Then came the longest five minutes of my life waiting for the doc to come in.

"Explain your symptoms again Mr. Leonard," the doc asked. "When I eat it burns/slight nausea feeling – diarrhea," Tony answered. "But his symptoms went away when he changed his diet to chicken and fish," I add.

"You're so young." Doc says. "Have you lost weight? No blood in your stool? No throwing up? No Loss of appetite? No cancer in your family?" "Not that I know of." Tony answered.

OK, I think to myself. Enough with the questions already what is it? "You're so young," the doctor repeats. "I want to do another endoscopy to confirm these results."

"What results?" I asked. The doctor paused. "What?... cancer?" Tony blurts out. The doctor nods, and says, "But you're so young," he mutters for the third time in as many minutes.

If there is anything I have learned it's that cancer has no prejudices! It doesn't care how old you are, your race, sex, or religion. It doesn't care, or respect, anything.

Hand in hand, with tears in our eyes, we walk out of that room, our lives, and the life we share, changed forever.

Let The Tests Begin

Tony's second endoscopy was conducted that Monday, February 6, 2012.. It was also the day they confirmed the leather stomach lining condition we now know as Hereditary Diffused Gastric Cancer (HDGC), or Linitis Plastica – a rare and aggressive cancer. We were immediately referred to the one of the best, (top one percent in the country) surgeons at Duke. Our appointment was in two weeks.

Tuesday: CT to see if it had spread.

Wednesday: CT results. Thankfully, it had not.

Thursday: Second set of Pathology results. Yup still cancer.

Now it's time to tell the rest of the family.

How Do We Tell His Mom...
How Do We Tell Our Kids?

"Cindy, sit down, we have something to tell you," we said to Tony's mother. Tony's eyes filled up with tears. Like me, Tony had also buried his only brother just a little over two years ago. "The results aren't good," he said. I think she knew because she said, "cancer," before we did. That's when we learned her father died of stomach cancer. But he was 78, not 39.

She cried, and said she would pray. That we would beat it...NO MATTER what.

To Anthoney (19), "Sweetie sit down. There is no easy way to say this. Daddy has cancer." Tears, tears, and more tears.

To Austin (11), "Hey baby, come sit down for a second. Daddy's sick. Daddy has cancer." After no facial reaction, "Austin, its OK to cry," First Austin cried. Then we both cried. I sat there holding him, assuring him we would get through it and Daddy would be ok.

To Alec (15), the hardest one of them all. Tony told him that he was sick. "How sick?" Alec asked. "I have cancer," Tony said. I don't think Alec ever cried so hard in all his life. I don't think my heart had ever broken for a child like it did that day. Alec went up to his room and started calling his best friends, the people he would lean on the most during these next months.

Now it was time to tell the rest of the family and our friends.

How I Told My Extended Family

February 10, 2012

Thanks to social media I managed to let my extended family know with one click of the "Post" button. "Good Morning Family!!!" I wrote. "I hate that I am having to use Facebook to share this news, but sometimes its easier than making a dozen phone calls. Some of you already know, but we received some sad news over the weekend, which was 90% confirmed Monday, and 100% confirmed yesterday.

"Tony was diagnosed with stomach cancer. He is handling the news as best as can be expected, however the boys are each handling it differently. Of course Aydin and Ashton have no idea, and we will keep it that way.

"Tony was having some stomach issues which we thought was an ulcer. During his upper GI they took some biopsies which came back positive. As a result they did a second procedure for a second opinion on Monday, being that he had no symptoms. Tuesday they did a CT of his abdomen which thankfully could not detect any cancer. Thursday morning we got the second set of biopsy results which confirmed the cancer.

"We believe we caught it very early being that his white blood cell count (WBC) is still normal and his symptoms are few. We have an appointment at Duke University Hospital which is #12 in the country for stomach cancer. His surgeon is Dr. Theodore Pappas who is one of if not the best GI surgeons out there. We will see him on 2/20/12 to get the official diagnosis. Stage, Treatment plan, etc.

"Most likely he will have surgery and chemo. Surgery will be done either 2/24/12 (Aydin's 4th b-day) or 3/2/12. I will be in Durham the whole time he is in surgery and in the hospital recovering.

"Now with tears in my eyes, I'm BEGGING you all to pray. Pray for Tony and PLEASE Pray for our kids. We already lost one person way too early, lets not lose another one. I will do my best to keep everyone posted.

"I love you all very much, and though I may not talk to you each and every day, I do think about you all always. There is a crappy 2 year anniversary coming up and I know we are all thinking of Mike. I am sure you can all agree with me that CANCER SUCKS!!! God Bless!!!

Love,

Christy"

Monday Feb 20, 2012

After what seemed like an eternity, we finally got to Duke and met Dr. Pappas who was awesome, answering all my questions before I asked.

"So how do we treat this?" he explained. "We remove the whole stomach. We connect your esophagus to your small intestine, remove the lymph nodes in the surrounding area, put in a JTube and go from there. You will eat six small meals a day instead of three large ones. Vitamin B12 shots for the rest of your life."

"Too easy," said Tony, as I'm still trying to swallow it all.

"How soon shall we do this?" Tony asked.

"No longer than three weeks," replied Dr. Pappas.

Dr. Pappas left, he to review the Duke Pathology report in order to decide when to schedule surgery. In walks his nurse, "OK." she said. "Looks like surgery is scheduled for this Friday. Pre-Op will be Thursday. Can you make it?" I scrape my chin off the floor. How am I going to get five kids squared away in two days? We nodded our heads, sure, sounds good.

On the way home, I called my sister Jaime who lives in Fayetteville. "How much notice do you need to take off from work?" I asked. My sister was my angel that day. She was there Wednesday night, went home and stayed all ten days we were gone.

Hit My Knees For The First Time in a Looooooooooooooong Time

February 24, 2012

It was the night before surgery. I don't think I had ever begged God for something in my whole life. And, I know I had never cried so much in 24 hours, EVER.

The alarm went off at 4am. We had to be there at 530. Before we left I got on my knees and prayed. All I could think to say was PLEASE PLEASE PLEASE don't take him from me, don't take him from my kids, don't take him...not yet...not now. Its not his time...YOU CAN'T HAVE HIM YET. With each falling tear, I felt a little bit better. Now it was time to wipe my eyes and put on a strong smile for Tony, time to head to the hospital.

The Story of the 8s

OK, so I'm a number's person.

I asked God for a sign and I got one The number 8.

Our four year old's birthday is 2-24-08; 2+2+4=8. He was 8lbs, 8oz and born at 6:20; 6+2+0=8
Surgery was 2-24 (Aydin's birthday); 2+2+4=8
Report time 0530; 5+3+0=8
PreOp Room #17; 1+7=8
Operating Room #26; 2+6=8
Surgery Start time 0800; 8+0+0=8
PACU Room #53; 5+3=8
Hospital Room# 6118; 6+1+1=8

I knew everything would be 8-OK.

Longest Hour Of My Life; Day of Surgery

February 24, 2012

It was 0700, the morning of surgery. I saw Dr. Pappas walk out of the PACU and gave him a big thumbs up. "It's going to be a good day today!!" I said, and he smiled and said, "Yes it is!"

Then I saw Thomasina, our wedding coordinator, walking towards me. I wasn't sure who it was at first, and then it hit me. I couldn't believe it. I wasn't alone anymore. I gave her the biggest hug and had the hardest cry – you know those cries where it seems no one is watching you and no one can hear you. The cry that comes from your belly through chest and out your mouth. It felt soooo good. I was blessed. God sent me another angel to help me. She took me back to see Tony before he went in.

Another surgeon came back to see us. Very straight forward, not the best bedside manner, but I didn't care, just save my husband's life. He and Dr. Pappas would be working together along with like 50 interns, 100 residents, and 1000 nurses.

"So I'm sure its been explained to you," he said to Tony. "This is some bad stuff you have. I want to be sure you understand that if it has spread outside the wall of your stomach, we are going to close you up."

"WHAT?!?!?! THAT ISN'T WHAT PAPPAS SAID!!! He said we were going to fight it no matter what!!!" I blurted out, standing up and stomping my foot. "There is no reason for him to go through such an extensive surgery if it won't help matters," he explained. "How far into the operation will you know if you are going to continue with the surgery or not?" I asked. "About 30-45 min," he responded.

The plan was to do it laparoscopically. They would look throughout his abdomen to see if the cancer had spread to any organs, and just get an overall understanding of what they were dealing with.

If his stomach was too hard, they would try via incision. More abrasive, but it didn't matter. Just getting the darn thing out was all I cared out. KILL THE HOST!!! Nevertheless, I would know an hour after surgery started if I was going to have the rest of my life with my husband, or just a few short months.

At 0730 they came to take him back. I kissed him, and told him I loved him. I smiled, didn't shed a tear and said, "I'll be here when you wake up." Surgery was going to be around two to three hours, but that first hour was key. I took the little pager Duke gave me for updates and walked out of the PACU, and burst into tears.

At 0745 Tony's mother, Cindy, showed up with Austin and Anthoney. My dear friend Terri was there, my shoulder to lean on. Terri helped keep the kids and my mother-in-law occupied while I worried myself sick. We went to the cafeteria, but I couldn't eat. I couldn't find the words to tell the kids or my mother-in-law what I had just been told.

Some of the families in the waiting room knew my situation. We all become like family, but no sense in worrying my MIL or kids. The pager went off at 0810, "They started surgery ten minutes ago Mrs. Leonard." "Thank you," I said. I looked at the clock. The 30-45 min window started.

I couldn't stop crying, I couldn't stop praying. No one knew what I knew. No one knew there was a possibility that Tony's stomach would not be removed. No one knew about that 30-45 min window. Terri took the kids and Terry's mother to the hotel. I returned to the waiting room. At 0900 I still hadn't heard anything. I went up to the reception desk and explained my situation. The called back to the OR. "Yes ma'am, I understand, I will let her know, Thank you," the receptionist said. My heart was pounding, no expression on her face. She looked up and me and smiled, saying the words I had prayed to hear. "They are continuing on with surgery!"

"REALLY? REALLY? OMG? PROMISE?" I blurted out. "Can I hug you?" She stepped around her desk, gave me a hug and I cried some more. She called Thomasina so I could share the happy news. All the family in the waiting room was happy and hugging me. It was wonderful. I had never been so relieved.

My baby was going to make it...we were going to beat this SOB!!

Four and a half hours later Dr. Perez came to the waiting area. "We got it," he said, "We got it all!!!" Of course we still needed to wait a week on pathology, but as far as surgery went...IT WAS A SUCCESS. OK, so they had to remove part of his esophagus, but so what? They got it all!!! They even did it laparoscopically. You couldn't get me to stop happy crying at this moment.

I told my mother-in-law and Terri, and started making phone calls! It was our little one's 4th birthday, and now Daddy would be there for his 5th, and many, many more to follow!!! GOD IS GOOD!!!

Nine Days At Duke

The next nine days were long. Tony was tired, in pain, but strong. The pain meds made him sleep. A LOT. It was like he hadn't slept in years. The boys and my mother-in-law came to see him Friday night, Saturday, and Sunday. You could tell Tony was in pain, and the boys weren't sure what to say. Tony was good at breaking the ice and getting them to lighten up a bit. Our nurses were great!! I got to stay in the hospital with Tony, and refused to leave his side. Cindy, and the boys went home Sunday around noon.

On Saturday his best friend Frank came to see him. That made Tony happy. Every day Tony got better and stronger.

Sunday: Lets take a walk. Tony started doing laps around the floor. His boss April, Curt, his boss's boss, and Paul, the office manager came to see him. That was BIG for Tony. You don't hear about companies caring for their employees to the point where they will come and visit them in the hospital!! But April, Curt, and Paul are special people, more than just bosses, they are friends.

Monday: TAKE THE CATH OUT!!! Poor Tony had a catheter that was driving him crazy. Luckily he had it removed on Monday and finally got a shower.

Tuesday: We got to see our babies!!! My sister Jaime brought Aydin and Ashton up to see us. I explained to Aydin about Daddy's boo boo. How he needed to be gentle. Aydin did very well seeing Tony, but it was really hard on Tony. Aydin was his little buddy, and seeing him brought tears to Tony's eyes. But, for all the tears, we were so happy that we had a chance to visit.

Wednesday: Tony got to start sipping clear fluids. He also received a special call from the Executive Vice President of his company, who even chatted with me. "Anything NCI can do," he said, "you just let me know!!" How super sweet of him and the company.

Thursday: We go the pathology report from surgery. There was still some cancer at the connection site, where the esophagus and small intestine met. It had also spread to his lymph nodes.

WHY GOD??? WHY??? ITS NOT FAIR!!!!!!!!!!!!!

"I am not leaving this hospital until I speak to an oncologist!!!" I demanded.

Just then there was a knock at the door. It was my sister with two caramel macchiatos from Starbucks©...MY FAVORITE!! She came!!! I didn't even ask her to, but she did. Some other friends of ours stopped by too, and they prayed with us.

Friday: MY MOM CAME!!! Appointments were made, doctors answered questions. We felt 100 times better. Time to fight this thing HEAD ON!!!

Saturday: We came home. Tony's boss April, and her family went grocery shopping for us.

There is no place like home.

Welcome Home

Wow, home sweet home...or was it?

Oh how nice was it to come home, our own bed, our own things...a shower!!! April was there with her family, putting away groceries. WOW! One less thing I have to worry about.

It was so nice to be home...but...Tony couldn't pick Ashton – who greeted him with a big hello – up and Ashton didn't understand why. Tony was tired and just wanted to lay in his bed. It was time to unload the truck, start some laundry, and set up Tony's tube feed machine. I now had to do everything they taught me in the hospital...on my own. Shots, flushing his tube every four hours, reminding him to drink fluids...but not too fast, hooking him up on his feeding tube and keeping the little ones away – all at the same time! Yikes!!

I don't think anyone can prepare you for that.

Just as I got Tony all settled in bed, there was a knock at the door. Terri brought dinner...YUM!! How kind of her. April with groceries, Terri with dinner. Careful, I could get used to this. All of our friends and family were so wonderful. My sister had done such a great job with the kids, I had to get them back in their routine and out of being spoiled. LOL!

I got my house in order, but now it was time to explain to the kids how important it was for Daddy to rest and not lift anything, how he needed to rest. And how I had to ask for a little bit more help around the house and with the kids. As it says in the Bible...and on the 7th day he rested. Yeah she rested...ME.

Patient Advocate

The day of Tony's CT, I started to stomp my feet again at Duke. Why haven't I heard from oncology? I am NOT going to wait until post-op to have these appointments that will take two weeks. I want to meet with them now. NOW DARNIT!! I wasn't sure what to do next except complain and threaten to go to another hospital until I heard from someone.

It must have been a blessing. On the way back from Duke we got a wonderful phone call from Brenda, our patient advocate. She was sooo nice and sweet and answered ALL of my questions. She let me talk and express my anxiety with cancer. She listened to my talk about losing Mike, (my brother who died of lung cancer at the age of 30 two years before, and how I couldn't lose Tony. I told her how I wasn't sure where we were supposed to go after surgery regarding oncology, and that I wanted everything to be ready to go with chemo, radiation, whatever needed to happen once he was cleared from surgery in two weeks.

The VERY NEXT DAY (Wednesday) Brenda called me with two oncology appointments for the following Monday; one with radiation, and one with chemo. I was happier than two pigs in $H!%. LOL

Finally, I was going to get all the answers to my questions.

What's The Plan Doc?

"Your CT looks great!!"

"SERIOUSLY?"

"We don't see any cancer on any of your organs," we were told. "The surgical pathology report said a bit of microscopic cells were left over at the connection site, but we can't see them on the CT."

This was the best news I had heard in a looooong time. So what's the plan? What next?

Chemo/radiation therapy – 25 rounds of it. 25 ROUNDS?!?!?!? Say again???

"For five weeks you will take your chemo pills at home and have your radiation done here Monday through Friday," the doctor said.

OH BOY...lots of driving, but my baby deserves the best and Duke is the best. Once that is done, it's three rounds of IV chemo – the one that will make his hair fall out. Hair shmair, it will grow back. Just get rid of the cancer!!

Come to find out they got this treatment plan from Japan where stomach cancer is more common and they have had pretty good results with this treatment.

"Too easy, when do we start." Tony said just as he did when they told him they were taking his stomach out.

Well, we started two weeks later, a week after post op.

My heart started racing. I had one more really hard question to ask. I wasn't sure how to ask it, but I really wanted to know. "OK, I have one more really hard question." I said, turning to Tony and apologizing for what I was about to say.

"Did we catch it in time? I asked. "When will we know?"

"We got his stomach out," the doctor answered. "So, yes. If we weren't able to remove his stomach we would be having a different conversation. When will we know for sure? We will know in 20 years."

"Great...I'll take another 20 years!!" I said with a big smile on my face.

She went on to tell us their goal was to kill any cancer cells left in his body so it won't attach itself to any organs. She explained how they would monitor him with CTs every three months, and Tony would get endoscopys every six to twelve months. OK, I can live with that. But, it wasn't me that would be going through the treatment physically, it was Tony. I just selfishly didn't want to be alone, or Tony to go anywhere. Again, Tony replied, "Too easy." Which always makes me smile.

Then it was off to meet our chemo oncologist who assured us this was the best way to go, and that Tony is young enough to get through the treatment...and that is what is important. So I had my new mission. I don't care how bad it gets, I would drag him by his hair if I needed to, and, of course, he asked me to ensure he finishes it.

So we have our plan, I know where to go next and I feel good. Right now I am smiling and cancer is going to LOSE!!!!

Post Op

Four weeks from surgery and Tony is doing great. "I feel great," he said, "I'm eating, sometimes the food gets stuck, but other than that so far so good."

The doctor had a smile on his face. He was thrilled to see how well Tony was doing. I asked him about where the cancer would come back, if it were to come back, and some other questions: How much can he lift? How about swimming with his Jtube (feeding tube)? How often will he have endoscopy's moving forward?

No swimming, but he can pick up Ashton now. A HUGE PLUS FOR ME!!! And as far as endoscopy's go, that decision will be made once he completes all his chemo and radiation.

All in all, the appointment went great and Tony was officially cleared to start his therapies.

Genetics - HDGC

HDGC WHAT???

Hereditary Defused Gastric Cancer.

OK, so I hear all this and I'm thinking...No, this can't be. Not my kids too? Please God, don't let this be the genetic kind. Please let this just be a fluke that promise me Tony doesn't have this gene. Because...if he does...and one of the boys have it, the only way to keep them from getting it is to remove their stomachs. *FROWN*

Radiation - Chemo Week 1

April 2, 2012

He's sick. He's not supposed to be sick yet.

The medicine isn't working very well. Thirty minutes after radiation, Tony feels sick.

"Welcome to being pregnant dear," I joke. But laughing is my only way to keep me from breaking. Sometimes I see this look on his face where he feels like he's going to be sick. How I wish I could take that look away..

Tony's mother had a heart attack a couple of days before his radiation started, and was in the hospital. I felt like I was being pulled in 20 different directions. If I wasn't at Duke, I was at Cape Fear. If I wasn't at Cape Fear, I was working. If I wasn't working, I was changing a diaper, or getting dinner on the table, or not doing a dozen things that needed getting done.

This was the first week of therapy, and I'm already thinking I'm not going to make it.

But, by Wednesday, my mother-in-law is home from the hospital, and Tony is getting used to the nausea.

Friday, Brenda got us another anti-nausea prescription so Tony wouldn't feel sick. They don't want him to be uncomfortable. They want him feeling good. Wait. It's Friday. We got through the week and the best part its Spring Break and my parents are coming. I will have some more help!!

That night, we got a very sad phone call from Tony's best friend, Frank. His daddy had passed away. He had also had a heart attack and had been in the hospital when his heart simply gave out. My heart went out to Frank and his family. Tony wanted to be there for him, but being sick, he was pretty limited. It seems everyone is sick these days. I have learned to have faith and that faith will pull you through no matter what.

It's what got and is getting me through all of this.

"Faith is not the belief that he can, but the knowledge that he will."
Anonymous

Radiation Took A Toll - Rounds 2-5

I have heard Long Island Ice-Tea's sneakily get you drunk. They kind of sneak up on you...and...BAM...you're hammered. Well, I would have to say Chemo-radiation does the same thing.

Everything was pretty standard. Get up. Get the little ones. Make sure the big ones were up. Load the car for our hour drive to Raleigh. Sit in the car with the little ones while Tony gets shot up with radiation – which takes all of ten minutes. Get the little ones dressed for school in those ten minutes. Then there's an hour drive back to Fayetteville to take the little ones to school. ALL BEFORE 9 AM!!!

This was my life for five weeks. The 5th week was so rough, I begged my mom to come down and help. She was great. She didn't just help, she gave me someone to talk to. I needed my mom and I needed a friend. Thank God she was there, and could be both.

HDGC Part 2

Genetics results: ITS NOT GENETIC!!!!!!!!!!!!!!

Tony's cancer isn't genetic, our kids are ok!!

Infusion

So this is the bad stuff from what I hear. But its only for a few days, nothing like having to take the Xeloda every day again. He has to WHAT?

Yup...EOX – Epirubicin, Oxaliplatin, and Xeloda. So the E and the O you get in your veins, and the Xeloda you take by mouth. You get three rounds of it, three to four weeks a part. No break from the Xeloda though, THAT one you take every day...twice a day...and the pills aren't small either. Poor Tony.

Counting the pills: one, two, three, four Monday morning. One, two, three, four Monday evening. One, two, three, five Tuesday morning...and so on...and so on...and so on.

My favorite? The biochemical warning on the box. Seriously? He's putting this in his body? Well back to the, "if it will kill it...I guess it's good."

Tony and the boys and Tony's best friend shave their heads. It was only a matter of time before Tony would too be losing his hair.

Screw It, We're Going To The Beach

Radiation is finally over. Now we have a three week break before the next wave of treatment, infusion chemo. So, I'm taking them to the beach.

I mean why not?

The kids deserve the break. I deserve the break. We need it before Tony gets sick again. So, I took the kids out of school for a couple of days and we went to the beach!!

We did the best we could.

Tony was still a bit under the weather, but at our resort I can let the boys go and have fun while I stay in the room with Tony.

We truly had a great time. Tony and I even got to celebrate our 5th wedding anniversary

Cancer WHAT? FREEEEEE!!

I am so proud of my four younger sons. Alec 15, has been my rock star. I tear up every time I think about how strong he was during all of this.

We never lost faith, and every time it was slipping for me, God put someone in my life to bring me back. The nurses at Duke prayed with us. Friends and family, the Pastor from our four year old's pre-school came by to visit. Tony saw me BREAKDOWN like no one in this town ever had. Everyone was just great!!! I took the past six months one day at a time, never stopping to think or else I would fall apart. Aydin's, "Dear God, make Daddy's boo boo better. Amen," is always a welcomed prayer in this house.

Tony had his post treatment CT on Aug 24, onemonth ago today.

IT WAS CLEAN!!!!!!!!

No lymph nodes! No cancer ANYWHERE. I swear it was divine intervention. God came down and cleaned Tony out. Every day my four year old would say, "Dear God, make Daddy's boo boo better, AMEN!!" I believe in prayer, and I believe that God has not only healed Tony, but healed our whole family.

We go to church now. We spend time as a family now. No more arguing, Tony is coaching Austin's (12) football team. He is still recovering from all the treatment and still has his feeding tube. But he's alive, and a new man.

GOD IS GOOD!!!

A Letter To Senator Burr
By Austin Leonard

Dear Senator Richard Burr,

My name is Austin Leonard and my dad was diagnosed with stomach cancer six months ago. He is 39 years old. I have two younger brothers two and four; and two older brothers 15 and 19 years old. When my family and I found out about my dad we were all scared. I was scared knowing that my dad is really sick and had to have his whole stomach taken out. He was going to have chemotherapy and other stuff. I was scared that I too could possibly lose my stomach at 21 years old. Either way I know my brothers and I, and our children, will have to get our stomachs checked every year for the rest of our lives. When my mom Christy and my dad Tony went to Duke Hospital my brothers and I had lots of questions like, will he lose all his hair, and did they catch it in time? Would I get cancer too? Could he still ride roller coasters? How long will he be sick? Lots of questions and very little answers.

My family and I are big supporters of cancer awareness. My football team and I were in the newspaper last year for wearing pink in support of breast cancer. When my dad was diagnosed, I noticed how little if any stomach cancer was supported. With us having to get our stomachs checked every year, what if I don't have the money to pay for it? Is there any support for me? How come the number two cancer killer in the world has little to no support or funding? Thankfully, November is Curing Stomach Cancer

Month. Will you wear a blue ribbon in support of my dad and my family? Will you help get the word out? Will you help raise money for research and medicine to help people like my dad? Please Mr. Senator, support my daddy's fight and those like him? Please help get the word out about stomach cancer awareness.

Sincerely,

Austin C. Leonard

Another Surgery

OK. So now the man can't eat. UGH! Enough already. Hasn't he gone through enough?

First they take his stomach so his whole world changes and now he can't swallow.

Scar tissue. Yup scar tissue.

His latest and greatest CT did in fact show his esophagus narrowing...FINALLY...we have the evidence we need for an esophageal dilation.

Sooo...it's back to Duke we go.

This time they tell us they are going to biopsy the connection site.

GULP.

I don't like biopsies. You know, I heard the word all the time before, and it never phased me...until this year. The good thing about it was that we would finally know if the radiation worked on Tony's cancer that was left over after surgery.

They never biopsied that area because nothing showed up on the CT, even though pathology said otherwise. This always made me nervous. But, I just filed it away in the back of my brain and continued to pray and put one foot in front of the other.

Back out to the waiting room, I open the work laptop and start to do what I always do during his outpatient procedures –

38

work...work...work. After about three emails, my pager goes off. He is done.

WOW THAT WAS FAST!!!

I walked back to his recovery room. Doc was there. No tumors, which is good, but, he did see the narrowing so he stretched his esophagus with a balloon.

Now my baby can eat!!!

The Results Are In - The "B" Word

Saturday, January 26, 2013

So...remember that B word I mentioned earlier? Yeah, *biopsy*. Typically not something I look forward to. I mean, Hell...last time I heard, "I think its an infection, and I took some biopsies which will tell us for sure," ended up not being an infection, but cancer. So, yes, I was a bit on the scared side when the GI doc at Duke told me he took some biopsies of his connection site during his surgery.

And...now...we wait. Wait a week for what? Our life to change? Too late! It already did, remember?

EMAIL: DUKE HEALTH. OK, so this is it – an email alert telling me some lab results are in.

I mean they can't be bad or else they wouldn't have emailed me right?

RIGHT!!!

And so I logged in and checked...hands shaking of course.

"The biopsies from your EGD were benign. Good news."

REALLY??? REALLY??? NO WAY...SERIOUSLY??? SOMEONE PINCH ME PLEASE!!!

A burst of emotions flushed through my body. The best way to put it is that it was relief like I had never experienced it before. I cried so hard. I mean, it was almost like waking up from a really, really, really bad dream. And happy tears. IT'S OVER! It was all just a dream. I know it wasn't, but now it didn't matter. It was over.

I ran upstairs to tell the boys. Forget Tony, the kids needed to know first. They looked at me like I had ten heads of course, because I had never told them we never really knew for sure that the radiation did its job. But they were happy, and promptly went back to playing XBOX. Even cancer will never stop the gaming in this house.

Then I came downstairs, crawled into bed with Tony and told him what the report said. I couldn't stop crying...I mean HARD crying. He told me he knew it would be OK; which is great, cause I sure as Hell didn't.

So, as we put the cancer behind us, and his dilation has been complete, it's time to focus on the next part of recovery...eating and weaning of the tube feed.

It's Been A Year

February 20, 2012

"Aydin baby, I'm so sorry, we are going to have to celebrate your birthday another time,"I say.

"Why mommy? No transformers?"

"I'm so sorry baby, mommy has to take daddy to the doctor so they can make him better, but Aunt Jaime and Uncle Zach will be here, and Ms. Hallie is going to celebrate with you at school with all your friends."

"OK Mommy," Aydin said with a sad, but no tears look on his face. "I, of course, cried and felt HORRIBLE. But surgery is scheduled for Friday, Feb 24, 2012, Aydin's 4th birthday. I had no choice.

February 24, 2013 – A Year Later

"HAPPY BIRTHDAY TO AYDIN, HAPPY BIRTHDAY TO YOU!!!!"

Not only was Tony there to see Aydin on his 5th birthday, but he was FINALLY cancer free!!!

A year from hell, but it was all worth it. Anything for Aydin and Tony on THEIR special day.

Damn Lymph Nodes

February 28, 2013

Why is it when things just start to look up, God likes to remind you to keep the faith and give you a reality check. I mean let's face it, life wouldn't be life without ups and downs...right?

Well, such is life. Tony had his CT today and, of course, I have to read the report before we get to Duke. These stupid phrases kept jumping out at me – like, increase in size, and cyst-like – then there are fancy words in front of organs like pancreas. All I can do is try to hide my eyes as they fill up with tears. Then I see it; lymph node increased from 1.1 x .7 cm to 1.3 x .8 cm.

I didn't do the math, i didn't convert centimeters to milimeters, I just saw increased lymph node and panicked. All I could think was, "Chemo again here we come Tony," followed by, "I don't care if I have to go through treatment all over again, we are fighting."

So, hand in hand, we finished our hour drive to Duke.
First stop: Urology. Yup so all these meds and treatments lowered Tony's testosterone. I of course thought it was fine, but noooo not that kind HAHAHA. Tony will finally find an end to his fatigue. Poor man! Tired all the time. No energy. Low testosterone. Low B12. Nerve meds making him tired. Pain when he eats.

Could it get any worse?

"The doc is going to insert some pellets in your butt cheek, in the mean time here's some gel," the doc says right before she says, "OK, let's examine your prostate."

BAHAAHHA! Poor Tony. I tried to rescue him by saying, "Look I have the radiology report. His prostate is just fine. Nope! Assume the position. Tony of course in his innocent tone asks, "How do you want me?" Just the comic relief I needed before we headed over to oncology.

We leave the doctors hand in hand and its off to get the results of his CT.

The doctor walks in and it's, "Why are you worried? I begin to cry and explain the report was bad. "So here's the break down," he said.

"*Cyst near liver*": Not really worried. It's not a mass. "– OK. Check!

"*Pancreas deterioration*," he read. "Of course, we radiated the heck out of it. Now the scarring is present on the CT." He explained it perfectly, "Just like a tattoo when you first get it versus a few months later after it's scarred." OK. Check!

"*Lymph Node increased from 1.1 x .7 cm to 1.3 x .8 cm*. Are we worried?" I asked. "Not yet," he answered. "It could be from the dilation. It could be the lymph node doing its job. It only grew by a millimeter, it's still really small. So, we scan again in two months to see. If its bigger, we PET scan and go from there. Until then, lets focus on his pain and B12." OK. Check!

Tony has been in pain so long it's now chronic and causing him to lose weight. So they changeed his medication, gave him his B12 shot, new scripts, and I was smiling. They increased his tube feed again so he would gain the weight back that he lost and said we would all touch base in a week.

It feels good to have a plan, get some answers, and understand what the radiology report means. Does it scare me? Hell yea, but am I a nut case? No. I am powerless over the results, but I can help Tony with the other stuff.

All in all, it was a productive day and we got a lot of answers. They will see us back in a month to check his T levels, B12, and weight. Until then, we keep on juicing and praying that the cancer stays gone.

Decreased In Size

Saturday, June 01, 2013

Decreased In Size! Decreased In Size! Decreased In Size! Music to my ears.

I kept reading those three words over and over again. Each time my heart would beat faster, the words got more blurry, and tears of joy ran down my face. It was going to be a good day!!!

The past two months have been stressful to say the least. I mean one minute you're wondering if the cancer is back and multiplying like crazy, and the next you are just grateful to have each other for one more day. Sometimes you just sit quietly and pretend not to know what the other is thinking, and other times you cry and fuss about the what ifs.

Lets face it...we are just normal.

Living life scan to scan sucks, but the truth is the key word there is living. I would rather live like this for the rest of my life than the alternative. Tony is a fighter and no matter what, he says he will beat this SOB or, as he puts it, "I don't have time for cancer."

Tony's A Survivor - His story

Thursday, May 08, 2014

My journey has definitely not been an easy one. No one can truly prepare you for what's ahead. No one can tell you how to live without a stomach, let alone eat. No one can tell you how to find a new normal. And, no one seems to know much about stomach cancer period.

Everything you read is bad. And, the more you research, the more scared you get. Let's face it, most people don't make it. But me, I decided this would be, "too easy...let's do it." My name is Tony Leonard and I am a still celebrating birthdays after my diagnosis of Linitis Plastica, gastric cancer Feb 4, 2012.

It was my 39th birthday and my wife Christy made me go to the doctor for an annual physical. She, of course, scheduled our appointments on my birthday. Happy Birthday right? I had also been feeling a little nauseous after I ate, but nothing major. My doctor referred me to a gastroenterologist to have a scope done to make sure I didn't have an ulcer. Due to the winter holidays I didn't get in until December. Upper GI was scheduled for January. I changed my diet and the nausea went away, so I honestly didn't think the scope was necessary, but again my wife made me go.

The morning of the endoscopy, the doctor came to us and pretty much gave me a clean bill of health. No ulcer, no hernia, no tumors – nothing. A slight irritation but nothing to worry about. "I like to eat spicy foods" I told the doctor. We laughed, shook hands, and it was back home. A week later Christy called me at work, and said the doctor wanted to see me Saturday morning at 8 am. She sounded a little worried, but you have to know my wife...she's good at hiding her emotions; (or so she thinks). The next day we went into the doctor's office and he went down a list of symptoms. I of course had none of them. No nausea no vomiting no burning or pain when I ate, no blood in my stool, no history of cancer in my family that I knew of. The doctor just repeated, "You're so young, you're so young." At this point I asked what it was Cancer? The doctor nodded and said yes. That Monday it was a repeat endoscopy, blood work and a CT the next day. I was referred to one of the top surgeons in the country at Duke in Durham NC. My wife demanded the best, and we got the best.

I got to Duke in less than two weeks, President's Day. The surgeon was great. He told me he was going to remove my entire stomach and connect my esophagus to my small intestine. "Too easy," I told him and asked him when he wanted to do it. Well little did I know that three days later was pre-op and that Friday was surgery...our son's 4th birthday. See, I have five boys and our youngest was a year and a half. I decided that I was going to beat this no matter what. Unfortunately though, the surgery was the easy part.

After surgery, my pathology report showed I had seven out of ten positive lymph nodes and there was cancer that had grown up my esophagus so they had to remove part of that during surgery. Two weeks later I was meeting with radiologist oncologists, chemo oncologists, and having more and more tests done. Twenty five rounds of chemo radiation (Xeloda/radiation) was horrible. The first three weeks weren't too bad, but weeks four and five were horrible. The docs were nice and gave me a three week break before three rounds of EOX chemo. Someone forgot to tell me I was going to be on chemo 24/7 for what seemed like six months. Just the thought of those Xeloda pills make me sick to this day.

When all the treatment was over it was time for scans. My scans were clean!!! I didn't have cancer. It was over!! One problem doc, I can't eat. See I had a feeding tube put in during surgery and that is how I ate during treatment. Food? Yeah no thank you. Throwing up when you don't have a stomach is like the worst dry heaving imaginable. So they had my esophagus dilated to help with the eating and food getting stuck. Two months later I had a lymph node near my pancreas grow, scare 1. Luckily it went down two months later. Three months later I was eating great, and maintaining my weight. Time to remove the feeding tube. I was on the road to recovery...was.

Just as things were going great, it was time for scans. What do they find? Sludge in my gallbladder. After an ultrasound, gallstones and sludge were confirmed and my gallbladder had to be removed. Too easy right? WRONG!! My intestine had adhered to my liver so that needed to be fixed, and I was hospitalized a week after surgery. I lost 40 pounds in a month and was getting weaker and weaker by the day. Christy started yelling to all my doctors until someone would listen. My oncologist brought me in right away. It was my heart. My pulse was in the 50s after walking around the oncology floor. I was admitted to the hospital again. Six weeks later I had a cardiac ablation. So now I still can't eat, my heart had to be fixed, docs can't get my meds right, and I am just sick and in pain and can't get out of bed.

Three weeks after the ablation, my feeding tube was put back in. When they got in there, they found that my intestine had wrapped around my esophagus and adhered to my abdominal wall. Sooo...that's why I couldn't eat...not. The surgeon of course fixed that, but I still had problems eating. Not only that, my feeding tube was causing intussusception in my small bowel and as a result they had to move it. The good news is there was not cancer, but my nutrition and "pluming" wasn't working to well.

Christy went back to my surgeon and begged for help. He started tests, brought in GI specialists, more tests and it was found I had diffused esophageal spasms. They are treating it with medication and soon I hope to be off my liquid diet. I went to a pain specialist and he has helped a great deal. He advised me that without a stomach I don't have acid to break down certain pills which is why my pain was so bad, half of the medication I was on wasn't absorbing properly. I'm grateful I have a pain doc that understands my anatomy.

So you're reading this probably going wow...scary stuff. The truth is cancer can be scary, cancer can be ugly. But as long as you have a strong advocate fighting for you and a great support network you can beat it. To think my life would be how it was before cancer is unrealistic. I do however get to spend every day with my wife and children. Our youngest is almost four, and our son whose birthday is on my surgery day, we share something special that no one can take from us. I get to watch my boys graduate from high school, and hold my granddaughter in my arms. I'm alive, and that is what matters. I'm not supposed to be, but I am. I am still learning my new normal and that is ok, because living is about life's lessons, cancer or not. I'm a survivor. I'm part of a club that unfortunately few are a part of. We have a very special unique membership. I encourage all of your stomach cancer patients out there to join.

My advice to you newly diagnosed patients, have a great advocate. Someone that can speak and fight for you when you can't. Ask for help and don't be afraid to ask questions and stomp your feet.

Really His Gallbladder?

October 2013

I have not written in a while, mainly because I just did not have time. Between Tony having four more surgeries, football, soccer, Alec having knee surgery, baseball, and...well...life, I've been a pretty busy mom. LOL

It was time for September scans and Tony had this funky pain in his belly. Scans show sludge in his gallbladder. REALLY of all things his gallbladder. Should have removed it during his TG.

By the time his ultrasound was done, it was full of stones. Surgery was scheduled for September 28. It was a Thursday. When they got in there however he had adhesions between his liver and intestine so they separated that. HA! The docs make it sound soooo easy. Well, I took Tony home and his butt was back in the hospital being admitted a week later.

His liver enzymes were elevated and it appeared he had a blockage in his bile duct. OF COURSE HE DID...because Tony cannot have a simple surgery without complications. The good news the blockage cleared on its own and Tony did not need another surgery. Well while he was in the hospital his doctor noticed some abnormal heart beats...little did we know there would be another issue down the road.

St. Johns!!!

November 2013

We went to St. Johns. What a great time we had. Or did we? Of course, we did, but Tony was getting sicker by the day. He had no energy, everything he ate made him sick, and he was throwing up when we snorkeled.

When we got back to North Carolina, Tony could barely get out of bed. His heart was acting funky, he could not stay awake, and I started screaming at his doctors until someone would listen.

Tony's oncologist told me to bring him in the next day. His nurse told me they had a bed waiting for him. Good thing. When his doctor was listening to his heart, he got a serious look on his face.

"C'mon Tony, lets go for a walk," he said.

He walked Tony around the cancer floor. After that walk, he hooked him up to the heart monitor and Tony's pulse was in the 40s. Normally, it is in the 90's/100's. Tony was admitted to the hospital right away.

They scanned him from head to toe. Atrophy of his organs from the radiation was apparent now. But, no cancer!!! His heart though, needed a fixin.'

During all of this, my 17-year old's knee got injured during the football playoffs and he needed an MRI. So while those results were coming in, Tony was in the hospital.

Tony was discharged on the Tuesday before Thanksgiving and we came home. Enough time to get Tony settled, showered and off to the orthopedics for Alec's MRI results.

Guess who needs surgery??? Yep. Alec had a 90 percent meniscus tear in his knee and surgery was scheduled for.the next day. Yep...the very next day Alec had surgery. So now, I have Big Baby #1 and Big Baby #2 out for the count and Thanksgiving dinner to cook.

Happy joy....NOT.

Thank God I had Austin. He and I looked at each other, fist pump. We got this!!

Cardiac Ablation

Tony went and had his heart halter put on after Thanksgiving. The results were what we thought. PVCs –Pre-Ventricular Contractions. Well, we can all have these, but, when you are having 30 a minute, or one every fourth and fifth beat, it needs to be fixed.

We met with the electrophysiologist and he explained how he would do the procedure. A catheter is inserted up his groin to his heart. They locate the area of the heart that is damaged, and pretty much kill it.

Too easy! Right? I think the hardest part was making Tony lay perfectly still for four hours after the procedure.

My friend Erin kept all the kids for us the day and weekend of the ablation so Tony could rest. We truly do have the best friends and support in the world – when I remember to ask for it. LOL

Well, now Tony's ticker is fixed. It's time for the next surgery, Endoscopy with biopsies and j-tube placement.

So Simple Yet So Difficult

Endoscopy with biopsies and j-tube placement. Must be the easiest, "surgery," out there. Especially for what Tony has been going through.

"How long will it take Doc?" I asked

"No more than 45 minutes. We'll see you in about an hour and a half," he replied.

Tick. Tick. Tick. Tick. Tick.

One hour. Two hours. Three hours.

Something's wrong.

Tick. Tick. Tick.

Buzzzzzzzzzz!

The pager goes off. FINALLY – three and a half hours later the doctor is ready to see me. Tony's gallbladder didn't take that long.

"Well everything went according to plan, I looked around we didn't see any cancer which is great. But, we did find something," the doctor said.

They sure did.

Tony's intestine was wrapped around his esophagus and had adhered to his abdominal wall!!!!!!!

Well, I'll be I KNEW SOMETHING WAS WRONG! Yeah, so they had to cut and pull and re-stitch and...ugh...

Can we just have a normal day? Just once?

Tony woke up from surgery in a ridiculous amount of pain and, unfortunately, it never went away. His feeding tube wasn't like the one before. He said the tugging was horrible and it felt like someone was shocking his insides.

A month later we were in the ER having his tube removed. "Why," you ask??? Intussusception in his small bowel. Yeah, while one doc said it was, "Nothing to worry about", his oncologist said, "That's what's causing your pain my friend."

Either way though Tony had his energy back, but the pain was just too much to bear. He couldn't walk, sit, stand, lay. It was just horrible.

Needless to say, the pain finally subsided when the tube came out, and then it was what seemed like back to Square One. So this time, I went to THE BOSS MAN...yep back to Dr. Pappas.

What The Hell Is A New Normal

Someone asked me once, what is your new normal?

Ha!! Funny!!

All I could think of was, I am married, I have five boys that drive me crazy, and a sick husband. That is nothing new, and certainly nothing normal.

Then I think back to our, "BC," days...Before Cancer.

Life seemed so much easier back then. Maybe it's because we didn't have our boys in their prime teen years, or maybe it's because our income was higher, you know...before disability. Tony and I did everything and went everywhere together.

Then in dawned on me. I did not feel like a single parent then. I catch myself now trying to handle everything with the boys by myself. I don't want Tony to get frustrated because that sure as Hell comes easier than it used to.

I've learned to accept that "Mother's Day," is just another day, and my birthday is a celebration that I too made it another year without checking myself into an insane asylum. Trust me, I've thought about it. I find myself taking on more now than I ever did before and I have no one to help me. I try to keep the day-to-day operations a smooth as possible for the kids without them seeing the stress, or the tears, but as the days go by, it gets harder and harder.

When people hear words like, "sick," or "cancer," their full attention immediately goes to the patient...AS IT SHOULD. But the family members and caregivers are often forgotten.

The kids' friends do not understand. Single parents do not understand. Only other caregivers understand. The problem is those other caregivers are so busy caring for their loved ones, who has time to talk?

Oh, and when we do talk, we sure as Hell are not talking about ourselves and our problems. We are talking about our warriors.

If you've ever been in this situation you know what I'm talking about. Please, do not ask how I am doing, because I am tired of crying. The shampoo got in my eyes, that is why they are red only works so often.

The new normal. HA!

Put one foot in front of the other and do the best you can.

If McDonalds is dinner, do not judge me. I promise I know how to cook. If my kids clothes aren't the latest fashion, do not judge them. Their stylish clothes may still be dirty. If we are having a bad day, there may not be a reason. And, I am allowed to have them. And, if I am tired, please just let me rest.

Welcome to *my* new normal.

Survivors Need Love Too

Well...just be grateful you are alive.

ARE YOU SERIOUS?

Be grateful that you live with pain?

Be grateful you have to take medicine that alters your personality?

Be grateful you can't eat at least one meal a day without it getting stuck?

Be grateful that you can make it to two out of ten of your kid's football games?

YES! Be grateful. The alternative is death.

The alternative is not being there for your children, because trust me there are children that would love to have their parents be at just one of those ten games.

There is a secret. Would you like to know?

If you are a survivor, you need love too. You will get a cold, and it is not the cancer. If you get the stomach flu, you would like to be seen by a normal doctor not 50 specialists. Woman still need pap smears. Men still need prostate exams. Hey Doc, why create a cure if you aren't going to bring the survivors back to reality?

"My throat hurts, Doc."

"Well...you need to call your oncologist, surgeon, GI doc, and Urologist.

Ummmm...my throat hurts...not my $*@&.

Whom are you kidding here? Do not tell me I am a miracle. I'm a survivor. I'm a fighter, a warrior that fought the hardest battle like any solider or marine. I get PTSD too. You know the smell of the chemo floor? Yeah, that triggers a memory. Every time I undress and I see the scars and holes in my body, I get a flashback. Please don't ask me to tell you about the side effects of chemo any more, I may just vomit on your floor, and PLEASE don't ask me to take another narcotic because the ones you gave me cause me to barley get out of bed.

I need you, wife, to tell me you still love me, I need you, friend, to come visit me, and I need you, doc, to tell me I WON the fight. Don't come see me only when I'm in the hospital. Come see me when I'm in my dark room, crying in depression because I can't provide for my family as I did before.

Don't only call me when my wife posts on Facebook that she's having a hard time with me and reaches out for help. Come...make me get out of bed. Let's go play golf. Don't be surprised when you see me, give me a hug. Let me give you advice. My brain isn't broken. Please know I'm still the man I was deep down inside, I just need you to help me find him again.

I don't want to be judged or fixed, I want to be loved. I want the parade for I have RETURNED from the battle of a lifetime. I want my life as it was before just like my family does. I just want to be loved, survivors need love to.

Esophageal Perforation

Tuesday, March 28, 2017

Monday March 20: Tony had a dilation done in his esophagus and a colonoscopy. Normally this is routine and we have a quick conversation with our GI doc and then its back home. I got to meet a great couple who are new to the journey. They were at Duke when we were. This trip, however, was different.

While Tony was waking up, our GI doc explained that there was an area of concern in Tony's large intestine. How concerned? He couldn't get the scope through his colon.

I was a little nervous, and then I heard three words that I had heard before; red, inflamed, and irritated. Those were the same three words I heard Jan 26, 2012 during Tony's endoscopy describing his stomach.

The lump in my throat began to form, while my eyes were welling up with tears. "Biopsies were taken and sent stat," I heard. But I wanted answers NOW!!! I took a deep breath and said, "Thank you," knowing the next couple of days would be long.

When we got home, Tony was in pain like I had never seen him in pain before. I assumed it was from the biopsies, so I gave him his medicines and put him to bed. After football practice I went home and Tony was asleep. I fed the kids and they showered and too went to bed.

Around 10:30 Tony was awake. This time he was calling for me in pain. I ran to him. He was white, sweaty, pale, and dry heaving. It was horrible. He started having difficulty breathing, so I called 911.

After some tests at the ER, we learned that Tony had free air in his abdominal cavity. This is life threatening and usually requires emergency surgery. The ER doctor contacted Duke immediately. Duke accepted a transfer from the local hospital to Duke. From this point on, the waiting game began.

THIRTY SIX HOURS LATER: Tony finally arrived at Duke. Do I go into how I called Duke transport and BEGGED them to come get Tony because Cape Fear Valley (CPV) was taking FOREVER?

Do I get into how CFV was only pumping Tony full of pain meds and antibiotics while waiting on Duke and he was not getting better?

If I heard, "I can't believe he's still stable" one more time, I was going to scream.

After a week in the hospital at Duke, we were happy to learn that the leak in Tony's esophagus had healed on its own. This was an answered prayer, because opening Tony back up was just way too risky of a surgery.

Each day we were at Duke however, I asked for answers to pathology from his colonoscopy. Unfortunately, every day was a, "No. Still pending. I'm sorry, nothing yet."

Sunday March 26, 2017: Tony was finally discharged...and pathology? Still no answers. But we got them the very next day.

The Phone Call...No Words...

Wednesday, March 29, 2017

I kiss him every day. I hug him. I argue with him. I get mad when he doesn't fix it. Why didn't he cook dinner? Why didn't he hold me last night? Why did he? All of these thoughts run through your mind when you are told it may be the last time.

All of it doesn't matter, just don't leave me.

That's just what happened at 1044 a.m. Monday morning when my phone rang. It was Duke. The call I had been waiting for. The call I had been dreading.

Pathology: Blah, blah, blah. Metastasis from the patient's known gastric carcinoma. In English – it's back.

After five years, Tony's stomach cancer has returned. How does this happen? How do I keep listening to the doctor? Why? All the questions come running back. The questions from five years ago are ringing in my head.

And then it dawned on me. Tony is now stage IV.

NOOOOOOOOOOOOOOOOOOOOOOOO!!!!!!!!!!!!!!!!!

I hand Tony the phone. I hear him pacing in the family room. Eager to know what the doctor is saying to him, I typed two words in the chat to my boss, "It's Back," to help refocus my mind.

Tony with tears in his eyes handed me the phone. I thanked Dr. Wolf for calling me and hung up. I went into the living room where Tony was. We threw our arms around each other and cried. We couldn't let go.

"Our love can beat anything," he told me.

I placed my hands on his face and made him PROMISE ME...PROMISE ME you will fight. PROMISE ME you won't leave me. PROMISE ME!!!

We started making phone calls, and then went up to his parents' house to break the news to them. Tony stayed strong, as his mother cried. I assured his mom and dad that we were fighting this NO MATTER WHAT!!

I could see tears in my father-in-law's eyes, but he was trying to hide them. I gave them each a hug and we went home.

On the way home I asked Tony, "How do we tell the kids...again?"

This time we decided to tell four of the boys together.
Once they were all quiet. I began,with, "There is no easy way to say this." I looked at Alec and Austin and I could see their eyes starting to water. "Daddy's cancer is back."

Just as I had expected, before I could finish my sentence, Alec ran upstairs. Austin threw his face in his hands and pulled his hat down over his eyes. Ashton and Aydin wrapped their arms around Tony as to never let him go. Ashton was crying so hard.

The two little ones are old enough now to understand what cancer means. Aydin even asked what stage he was. I stood up and went to Austin and put my arms around him, while Tony held the little ones.

Alec came downstairs and went outside. Before he did, I hugged him and told him WE WILL get through this, and then he left. Tony and I swapped kids. I went to the little ones and he went to Austin. Austin collapsed in Tony's arms.

Now the five of us were crying. Sometimes, that's all you can do.

I promised the boys that once I knew something, I would tell them and keep them posted. Tony told the boys to get the guns and to go outside and shoot their frustration out...and so they did...except Aydin. He went into the office. When I went in there, he was researching stomach cancer. He wants answers, as we all do. I just wish he didn't have to deal with this at the age of nine.

Regardless of the tears, we are a strong family and have been through a lot. We have our ups and downs, but when crap hits the fan, we are stronger than ever.

And Monday, I had to be the strong one for five boys and their daddy.

The Visit

Just one month ago, Feb 24, we were celebrating Tony's five year canversary at Luigi's.

My mom lifted her glass to a toast, and Tony thanked everyone for standing by him while he was nothing short of an asshole some days.

Sorry Baby...but you were. Ha Ha!!

Lots of hugs and smiles, periwinkle ribbons and love in the room. It was also Aydin's 9th birthday. The two share such a special day. Tony made it. He's a miracle and blessed, and it was time to start living again.

The next day we were off to DC to lobby for stomach cancer research. Tony only made it to half the meetings. He was nauseated and in so much pain. I finished the meetings with a different group of people. We did however meet with Senator Burr (R-NC). We thanked him for his letter to the NIH last year and had quite the nice visit. He and Tony talked more about football and lacrosse than they did stomach cancer, but boys will be boys.

A week later Tony and I went to meet his GI doc. Again great visit. This time however, Tony asked for a colonoscopy as well as an endoscopy. He had both procedures 11 days later, and we heard there was a possibility of the cancer being back. That same night Tony was in the hospital with the perforation.

The following week, we learn the cancer has returned and its straight to Duke.

Walking into Duke this time was all too familiar. Except this time, there weren't smiles. This time it was looks of sadness, tears, and shock.

No one could believe what they were reading. No one could believe it was back after five long years. This time they didn't call our name.

Instead our nurse walked over to us, patted us on the back and asked, "Are you ready?" in a soft tone. We got up, went into the room, and began to share the events of the last month.

When our oncologist walked in he sounded up beat, but confused. "I didn't want to see you guys again for this," he said."

Ugh! Like we wanted to be there!

I started to tear up, and he asked what was going on and what symptoms Tony had. I shared that this is why I was so damn frustrated at doctors blaming the other doctors. CLEARLY something was going on. And…was I ever right!!

Between the edema in his legs, the bile, not being able to use the bathroom, the extreme constipation, the pain in his left side – all cancer symptoms of the cancer, but being blamed on something else – the doctors were losing sight of the big picture.

He ordered a PET scan which we had to get in the next couple of days. I kindly told him he would be getting it this afternoon. He chuckled and said, you could try.

HELLO…do you know who you are talking too? Yes, we got it that afternoon.

"What's the plan doc?" I asked?

"*If* the PET scan shows it's contained, I'm going ask for the tumor to be cut out," he ssaid.

"What about chemo?" I asked.

"I don't know Christy. It didn't work the first time. Which means it won't work now." the doctor replied.

"BUT IT GOT US FIVE YEARS!" I reminded him

I really didn't like this plan. Not one bit.

I emailed all the doctors on our medical advisory board from Debbie's Dream Foundation. I was *not* going to sit around and wait, I had to have my second, and third opinions.

"Are we stage IV now?" I asked. I just *had* to hear it from a doctor. I mean...I knew the answer already. I just had to hear someone said it out loud.

"Christy, it's back in a distant organ...yes," the doctor said. "But that does not effect treatment, so it doesn't matter."

I liked that answer.

So here we are in the waiting game. We will go back to Duke in four days, if I can't get there earlier.

Tony's PET scan should be viewable now and we should know if surgery is an option for Tony. I refuse to sit around while Tony has cancer inside of him doing whatever the Hell it wants to do when I could be stomping my feet and pressing for surgery. Besides, I already emailed his surgeon just in case. I've already received feedback from the DDF doctors that are on standby ready and willing to help.

In the meantime I will continue to wait, and pray, and do things that keeps my mind busy.

I will kiss Tony a few extra times today.

Hug on him a little more.

And, add a few more things to the, "Honey Do," list.

After all, we still have to live, and so does he!!

My Little Boys Have Feelings Too

Monday, April 10, 2017

I wish my youngest Aydin and Ashton knew their daddy before he was sick.

I wish they knew his laugh, his smile, his jokes. I wish they knew him when he coached, I mean really coached. I wish they knew his love and gentleness.

But they only know a daddy who is sick. A man in pain, short tempered. A man who is scared just as much as them.

Tonight I see two small boys, six and nine, terrified of having their daddy sick forever. Two boys who wish they knew their daddy before cancer. Two ANGRY boys that don't think any of this is fair. Two boys lashing out at the world when they don't get their way. Because of, lets face it, the small things they don't get.

Tonight at Ashton's ball game, I watched Tony cheer Ashton on and get frustrated when he wouldn't listen to the littlest instruction. I watched Tony's heart break and pain in his eyes.

I don't talk a lot about what the youngest are going through, but they are hurting. They are sad. They are angry. They just want their daddy.

Is that too much to ask?

So tonight, they will stay up late, curled up in daddy's arms and cry themselves to sleep.

I am Just As Scared

I have never really shard all the emotions that go through my heart during the journey. The fear, the strength, the love, the tears, the joy, the sadness...and oh...the ANGER.

Am I wrong for being upset and angry at cancer? How DARE it come in and ruin my perfect little family? How DARE it test my faith and my vows of sickness and health? HOW DARE it pain my children and keep me from being the mom I have ALWAYS wanted to be?

I'm just as scared as them, I'm just scared as you, I'm afraid.

And sometimes, even though everyone is here for me, I feel alone. Sometimes, I just need to cry,or scream at the top of my lungs. But, if I express that anger or show a glimmer of fear, who will be there for my children? Who will dry their tears? Who will show them that we will be OK?

I have to love them all through each and every one of their emotions. Whether its anger, frustration, fear, confusion, happiness, all of it, I, Mom, must love them through it.

And...oh...it's so hard.

I'm scared that my fear will show, and leak out and they will lose faith. I'm scared that I will join the young widow club. I'm scared that the surgery won't be successful, I'm scared the chemo won't work, I'm scared of missing out on my young children's lives.

I FEAR THE UNKNOWN.

Dry your eyes you're told.

Be strong for them.

You aren't alone.

He'll beat it.

Y'all got this.

I'm here for you.

Yet, I just want to be a little girl where my parents tell me its going to be OK, and it is. I want my mom to be able to kiss his boo boo and have all of it healed. But, it doesn't work like that.

I have to keep holding on. I have to stay strong for my warrior, my kids, his parents, everyone. And, deep down, I'm just as scared of the rest of them.

Don't you get it?

GOD DO YOU HEAR ME??????

I'M SCARED!!!!!!!!!

Please Lord give me some courage to fight this fight with him. Take away my children's fears and my fears. The tears are flowing ever so hard now. It's the night before surgery, yet one more surgery that will be determing life or death.

Tonight I will cry. I will hold him. I will hit my knees and pray. YOU CAN'T HAVE HIM YET! Tonight it's okay to be scared. Tomorrow, though, I MUST BE STRONG!!!

The Scan Was Wrong

The night before surgery a little request to our surgeon...

"Dr. Pappas,
Thank you again for everything you have done for Tony and believe
it or not our family these past five years. It's time for another miracle.
I will be praying for you and your team tomorrow. If we have to do
this every five years I'll take it. Please do everything you can tomorrow
to help Tony!! Please save him again!!
All my best!!"

These boys deserve a father to watch them grow up.

Report time was 8a.m. A prayer with Pastor Sammy and his wife. A visit with my mom. And a last minute visit with Frank, Tony's childhood best friend.

I kissed Tony goodbye as they rolled him into surgery. There are fewer tears this time. I had been through this before. I knew what to do. The best part...I wasn't alone this time. I didn't have to watch the clock by myself.

Tick. Tick. Tick.

Instead I had conversation to keep me occupied. I didn't have a brain left to its own dark devices. I had prayer. And I had hope rushing through my head and heart.

Exactly one hour after surgery started, I went up to the desk and asked the lady – a familiar face from five years before – to call back to the OR and ask for an update. She revealed they were continuing on with surgery, and making the incision now.

Happy and relieved, I walked back to the group and shared the good news. Now it was another two hour wait.

What would be next?

Instead of waiting I decided to give the good news to Alec that surgery was continuing. He must have been watching the clock because he called me just ten minutes before for an update.

Three hours later, my pager went off. Dr. Pappas was ready to see me. I went into the room by myself and sat down on the couch. I watched the clock, just as I started counting, Dr. Pappas walks in the door and tells me everything went well.

With a calm voice he tells me what all he had to do, what the cancer had done, and what was next. He told me this was good news, and I needed to get myself together because I would be the first person Tony would see when he woke up.

This is as good as it gets.

I walked back out to the group, trying to keep my emotions contained. Happiness. Fear. Anxiety; all rolled in one confused feeling.

"Dr. Pappas did it again!!!" I announced

Knowing that any other surgeon would've closed Tony up, I was even more emotional. Why all this if the tumor was only in his colon?

IT WASN'T.

When the doctor got in there, the tumor was growing through his spleen, pancreas, and colon. The scan was wrong. Thank God though, because they continued with surgery. First the colon in chunks to get back to the pancreas and spleen. Bye Bye spleen. Bye Bye tail of pancreas. And Bye Bye 23 centimeters of colon.

My love, my best friend, my soul mate has a long recovery ahead. But he's still here. He, and we, will continue to fight. I have some good news for my babies!!!

Thank God for answered prayers.

Cape Fear's Austin Leonard Surprises Dad at Duke Before Prom

By Jaclyn Shambaugh (Fayetteville Observer)

Tony Leonard was a little more than a day removed from surgery to remove a tumor in his abdomen.

Cape Fear junior Austin Leonard, a part of the Colts' state runner-up football team in the fall, knew his father, Tony Leonard, wouldn't be home to see him off before his first prom Saturday. Tony, little more than a day removed from extensive surgery to remove a tumor in his abdomen, is in recovery at Duke.

No problem. Austin and girlfriend Bobbie Machelle Cox took prom to him. "Austin asked if him and his girlfriend could get all dressed and come surprise him," said Christy Leonard, mother to Austin and four other sons with Tony.

"Take prom to him."

The couple donned their tux and gown and showed up Friday in Tony's hospital room, giving him a chance to see Austin and Bobbie in their best a day before Cape Fear's prom.

"It was Austin's idea but Bobbie's mom, Heather Smith, made it happen," Christy said. "It still makes me cry when I think about it. Tony was hiding his tears last night when he saw Austin."

The Leonards have been advocates for stomach cancer awareness since Tony's initial diagnosis in January 2012. The couple organizes an annual golf tournament, Debbie Dream's

Foundation Golf Tournament, to raise money for stomach cancer research.

Through their efforts, North Carolina legislators have declared November "Curing Stomach Cancer Month" three straight years.

Tony has had multiple surgeries, including the removal of his stomach a month after his diagnosis. During his most recent surgery, performed Thursday, doctors removed his spleen and parts of his pancreas and colon to remove the tumor.

"It's going to be a long recovery," Christy said. "But I think this might be a prom that will never be forgotten by Austin or Tony."

Credit:http://www.fayobserver.com/sports/20170506/cape-fears-austin-leonard-surprises-dad-at-duke-before-prom

10 Days At Duke...AGAIN

The walls all too familiar.

The linens haven't moved.

The nurses' faces are the same as before.

You're happy that the shower you got this time has a shower head that stands up straight.

There is still pizza in the cafeteria, and the 24/7 Starbucks means you might just put on a few extra pounds this week or two.

The stories are still the same of the loved ones that had a life saving surgery,.

And, the parents are still praying for their child with cancer, praying that he or she can make it through the next round of chemo.

We all are praying.

We all hurt.

We all walk the same halls and share the same stories.

Friday Day 2: "Come on honey, it's time to get up and walk," I say, trying my best not to sound like his mother, but an encouraging wife begging for her husband to recover just as quickly as he did the first time.

A simple request of extra pain meds for your hubby because you know what will get him through the next 48 hours.

"Baby, its one day post op. Don't you want a shower?"

"NO!!"

Still having to smile. Still having to encourage, but not nag. You finally get him up and in the shower. This time though, he wears out quicker than before.

He's in more pain.

A 12 plus inch incision and three manipulated organs just causes more complications and requires more TLC.

Will I survive this too?

Friday Night: Surprise prom is here at Duke as Austin and Bobbie walk the halls to visit dad, followed by happy tears, and hugs.

Life is only going to get better and your family is here for you, proven once again.

Saturday: WHERE ARE HIS MEDS????

It's not the nurses fault, The pain doc ordered WHAT??? Dear God, that's PCP!! No wonder he is seeing purple elephants and pulling away from my hand.

NURSE HELP!!!

They ordered too much!! Can he just get some Tylenol? I promise it takes the pain away? IV, yes. I don't care who that guy is, he doesn't know my husband!!! Finally a meeting with surgeon, pain management, and pharmacy.

I don't care what you want. This is what we are going to do. You switch him to NPO, you order IV Tylenol and switch the Dilaudid to Fentyl and turn down the damn PCP.

The cocktail I requested worked!!

In 24 hours Tony is up and walking. He's showering. Sitting up. The pain is down to a six. AMAZING!!

Now the cath comes out and waking up all night for bathroom trips and writing urine counts on the board. The sleep deprivation starts.

But I will stay strong, I am here for him. I will NOT have it any other way. I will make it through no matter what we go through this week.

Sunday: A visit from Alec, and his girl friend, Mackenzie, and her family.

Tony got up and walked around after he got his dose of Alec. Followed by a very excited nine and six year old that missed their mommy and daddy, "so much."

Dinner in the cafeteria and evening coffee in Starbucks with my dad and mom and hot chocolate for the "L'il A's".

Tears and hugs when its time to say good bye, because this sure as heck never gets easier.

Monday - Day 5: Third sheet change, The blankets are still in the same cabinet. The cups and ice chips are around the corner from the nurses station. We get smiles and cheers on the second lap around the floor.

Then the miracle we needed; Tony POOPED!!

It took a few days, but it finally happened. The colon is working and we are closer to going home.

Tuesday: A childhood friend surprises Tony. Broin came by and made Tony get up and walk three laps. He is here to push and encourage, so I can take a break. Seeing his friends perked Tony up and makes the journey just a little bit easier and worth a little bit more.

Wednesday: MOVING DAY!! We got moved to a bigger room because our toilet was messed up. But...does the shower work? It's so important that I get my daily showers.

Thursday: More visits from another childhood friend and former co-workers. Frank and Jim came by along with another dose of Alec. More laps around the floor. IV's are slowly being disconnected. Home meds are being introduced. Mood swings are in full force.

And me? I'm just excited that my love is FINALLY ready to get the hell up outta here!!

By Friday we are discussing discharge to be home in time for our baby's football games and Mother's Day.

Tony is able to keep food down. He just needs to get on the protein and high calorie diet.

Too easy.

This isn't our first rodeo.

Pack up time for discharge. Ready to go. Just one final night in the recliner. One more time to the familiar cabinet. One more night in this room. One more walk through the halls.

Saturday Morning: Dr. Pappas unexpectedly orders vaccines, delaying discharge a couple of hours,.

I thought one more walk through the halls. One more visit to Starbucks. One more story being seen by the walls. It's time to go home and surprise our babies!!!

Finally, happiness! Duke in our rear view mirror...only to have us return...again *CRY*

The Balance of
Caregiving / Mom / Wife

Tuesday, June 06, 2017

Our first week home from Duke was exhausting. Mother's Day was a day of cleaning and spending time with the little ones who missed us dearly. I promised them we would be there for baseball games this week and the big Championship football game that Saturday.

FINALLY we were home.

This means I have to do the packing, adminster the lovinox shots, remind Tony to eat, and remind him to take his meds.

When the alarm went off at 6:00 it wasn't because the doctors were making rounds, it was because the boys had to get up for school. And the 8:00 a.m. alarm meant back to work. There was no Starbucks to make my coffee, it was back to the grind.

I was back to my new normal...whatever that is.

Monday the nurse came and packed Tony's wound for me. She assured me she would be there three days a week and I could call her ANYTIME.

By the second visit we were getting concerned that Tony's wound was not healing but getting bigger. Staples were popping off.

Is this normal, I wonder as I snap a photo from my phone and email it to his surgeon. Keep packing and watch it they say. By the third visit, day Tony's wound looked HORRIBLE. It was bigger, deeper, and you could see his internal stitches.

The term DEHISCING was used. Whatever the heck that is. Is that even a word? I asked. Apparently it is. It meant Tony was overdoing it because for the first time in YEARS his deep pain had started going away and he wasn't nauseous. Well God has a sense of humor. He forced Tony to lay on his butt and get back in the bed.

On Friday, we snapped another photo of the incision and immediately got a phone call from Duke.

Tony was being directly admitted back into the hospital that day and needed to be there in the next couple of hours. I asked Alec to go check the little ones out of school. They were so excited to walk in the door at 1:30 instead of 3:30.

Big hugs and kisses.

"Boys sit down." I said

"What is it mommy?" Aydin asked.

"Daddy and I have to back to Duke."

"WHY?!?! FOR HOW LONG???" Aydin shouts with tears in his eyes.

His anger has been only getting worse when it comes to cancer and his dad's illness. I don't have the physical strength to even hold him anymore. This big nine year old football player doesn't have any idea how to control his emotions and, as his mom, I have NO CLUE how to help him.

Then the baby.

He just puts his head down and jumps in my lap and says, "Mommy, who is going to take care of me?" "Boys, I said, "I think its just for a few days. Daddy's boo boo isn't getting better, so they need to get it checked out so he doesn't get sick." I told them it would be OK. and I would call them in the morning.

Next, I called my mom and said, "GUESS WHAT MOM!!!"

Tony and I get the weekend to ourselves, no kids, and out of town to celebrate our 10th year wedding anniversary.

Yep, back to Duke we go. I told her that Alec had the boys and Angie was on stand by. And of course I too would keep her posted.

"MOM!!! MY GAME!!! YOUR GONNA MISS MY GAME!!!" It was the county championship and I would have to get updates from Facebook.

I AM SO SICK AND TIRED OF MISSING BIG EVENTS!!! And now my kids are too.

When the team at Duke heard about our anniversary they got us the big room and a big piece of chocolate cake to celebrate. It's the little things that make this journey a little easier. Luckily Tony only needed a wound vac and not another surgery. I went down to the gift shop and got Tony a little anniversary something and a card. I insisted on celebrating one way or another.

The next day I got the updates on how great the team did. Not one mistake was made and Aydin had some great hits. Everyone on the team snapshotted photos of Aydin with the trophy and sent them to me.

I thought it would make me happy. Instead I cried. Another nail in the coffin of missed events that CANCER had taken away from me.

Sometimes I feel like I have to choose.

But, why should I have to choose between my boys and my husband?

If I am supporting Tony, I feel like I'm neglecting my sons.

If I'm supporting my sons, I'm neglecting my husband.

What they don't all realize, I'm here. I'm there. I'm everywhere. I'm in everything they do and, though they may not see it or can touch it, I PROMISE I'm supporting all of them. I just wish they knew how much I love all of them and at the same time how much they are ripping me apart.

Sometimes I feel like I want to smother my warrior with a pillow when I'm mad at him for not disciplining the kids for me and frustrated because I just miss my husband that held me and told me it would be OK. I need his arms around me, holding me tight.

Now I have to share those arms with the boys who just want the strength of their father. It's all a balance. It's all a challenge.

But, at the end of the day (Monday), when we came home from Duke, the boys tackled us with hugs and kisses, the older boys hugged us with relief, and my husband kissed me good night in our own bed. As I locked the doors that night, I looked around the quiet peaceful house and thought to myself that I sure wouldn't trade this for the world. That was my balance. Life wobbles, but at the end of the day it all levels out.

One Minute Its in His Liver, The Next it's Not

There is nothing worse than getting a scan and reading the report and seeing the word...METISTATIC.

It always makes your heart drop, eyes fill up with tears, and puts a lump in your throat so big you feel if you swallow your saliva you might just throw it up, because it won't go down.

Tuesday afternoon was just like that.

The radiology report we received suggested Tony had metistatic disease in his liver. This meant only five weeks post-op, Tony's cancer was spreading. I didn't even know how to react. My emotions put me in a depression I had never felt. I couldn't believe this was actually happening.

Sitting the boys down was the hardest part.

Aydin asked me if Daddy's cancer was back when he saw me crying in the car on the way to therapy. All I kept thinking was, will he even make it to Christmas? I didn't know what the Hell I was supposed to say, how I could possibly stay strong. Then of course I shared the news with the other boys and their tears broke me.

I emailed Tony's surgeon immediately.

"TONY'S CANCER IS SPREADING," I put in the subject line. Dr. Pappas emailed me back right away requesting the CD. I already had it sent via overnight so Duke could take a look at it.

Wednesday afternoon my phone rang. Duke Radiology had already read the report. THEY DISAGREED WITH THE

REPORT!!! They said NO EVIDENCE OF DISEASE at the liver!!!

Apparently the blood was flowing funky which can appear to be tumor like in appearance. Now the question was who do I believe?

Friday couldn't come fast enough.

We met with Tony's new oncologist and she too agree with Duke's report after she reviewed the scan. "We will run some tests on your tumor to determine whether we start you on immunotherapy or chemotherapy," she said. "In the mean time, Tony has to get his strength back."

We have six weeks to get him strong. We don't need any more delays in treatment.

While this is great news, greeted with a sigh of relief, it's hard to not have some anxiety about cancer floating around in his body with no course of treatment keeping it at bay. But then again, its about quality of life as well.

We will get to enjoy the next six weeks!!!

HELLO SUMMER!!!!

I'm Cooking As Fast As I Can Dial

Friday, June 23, 2017

OK. It's Friday night. I had a long week at work. It happens. It was nice actually. No trips to Duke. No scans. Just a normal work week.

What the heck is that like?

It means it's Friday night and I'm cooking just as fast as I can dial cause I sure as heck don't feel like pulling out the pots and pans. Do you have ANY IDEA how good it felt to order pizza and pasta and not have a reason other than I felt like it? It was like a sigh of relief.

There doesn't always have to be a CANCER reason, sometimes it can be a NORMAL reason. Like happy hour at 5:00 will still go on whether chemo is going on or not. Actually, come to think of it, my brother did order pizza and had it delivered during his chemo.

I called Alec and whined, "Whatchya doing?"

"You fly. I'll buy."

Too bad he was playing basketball. So we decided on delivery. Not much to order for takeout that's delivered. Ah...the joys of being in the country.

So Pizza Hut it was.

Tony actually came to the table tonight. He's so frail, but all the matters to me is that we still have our family dinners. Sometimes family dinners are in the bedroom and that's OK. too.

The rules can change at the drop of a hat and THAT IS OK!!!

Sometimes the laundry piles up and sometimes I order take out. Cancer or not, don't we ALL feel that way sometimes?

I'm cooking just as fast as I can dial, has to be my favorite Post-It note. My sister Kathleen would agree. Sometimes life just happens so fast we have to take shortcuts. I wonder who invented the word shortcut and why. It's called making life easier and who ever said it had to be hard? It's really what we make it to be.

And rules?

What rules? That's all up for discussion.

Maybe I should come off my soap box now and laugh, smile, and say, you know what?? Today was a GREAT DAY!!! TGIF! Today I will smile and feel GREAT about it!!

Survey Says....

What a few weeks it has been. From there being a possible lesion on Tony's liver to maybe not. Tony has been super sick and he isn't able to keep anything down. My tears have been flowing harder than ever. I feel like I'm watching the love of my life drift away right before my very eyes and I can't stop it. He is pale. He is weak. His cheeks are thinning and his bones are more visible than they've ever been.

A great conversation with our nurse at Duke had me realizing the one thing I have always wanted during the past 10 years Tony and I have been married. That's to be married in the Catholic Church.

It's a bit of a process when you've been married before, but it means a lot to Tony and he promised me a long time ago he would make it happen.

Then cancer had to go and infest our lives but I never thought there would be a death sentence at the end of our cancer journey.

Hope. They tell you to keep the hope and faith and not to ever give up. However, when your loved one is Stage 4, its soooo hard not to imagine what may come sooner than you had ever feared.

I am just so tired of crying, ya know? I'm so exhausted from it. I learned that blasting the radio and driving at 70 mph screaming at the top of your lungs helps. I've learned it's OK to let out that deep hard-in-your-chest cry. Besides...no one can see you. Hopefully their eyes are on the road. If not, I've got more problems.

Before you know it, it's scan day and...drumroll...wait ...stop...hold tight. The insurance company has suddenly decided they "need" a peer-to-peer to discuss why they should pay for a cancer patient's CT scan.

Thank you CIGNA who denied three years worth of scans for making this hard

Thank you CIGNA for lettting his cancer return, undetected, in three organs which we couldn't catch any earlier.

Thank you CIGNA. Thank you!

So yes CIGNA I am not surprised that you would suddenly "need" to discuss his case with his oncologist.

Oh CIGNA, your poor shareholders want their profits. That's why you will only approve the brain CT *if* they add contrast to it. OK. CIGNA I get it! It all makes sense. You've been up nights worrying about ways to spend more money.

At least we have one thing in common

Well, three hours later, CIGNA said it was OK. to see how my husband's cancer was doing; and we got the CT done.

What was the verdict you ask? Cause YOU KNOW I already read the report.

The spot on Tony's liver has disappeared. This means there is *no* question about there being a metastasis to his liver!!

The spot on the pancreas has thinned out a bit and has been determined to be a lesion from surgery. In other words, NO EVIDENCE OF DISEASE!!!

This is the best type of scan a cancer patient can get. In Tony's case however, that doesn't mean much, because his cancer doesn't tend to show up on scans. We still know there *is* cancer in his colon and pancreas. It's just a matter of keeping it under control with the maintenance chemo he will be starting.

The truth for a Stage 4 cancer patient is, good news is anything but growth. We like words like, "stable", "shrink", and, "no evidence."

We know we will be living with cancer forever. But for today we are alive. We are blessed. And, we are grateful to spend another day with our loved ones.

Why do I say we as the caregiver? Beause my warriors fight is my fight. And because his life is my life too. We are in this together and we will be to the end – whenever it comes and whatever shape it takes.

Time For Poison

Here come the Hazmat suits. Does ANYONE else see something wrong with this picture? I mean really, why is it alright for Tony and me to sit there in our regular clothes when the nurse needs full HAZMAT to enter the room?

And, what is that she's holding?

Ah yes. Chemo the medicine – poison – that will save my dear husband's life. Or that is the plan because we can't just sit there and do nothing. And it worked before.

So here comes the medicine in an IV bag with a big HAZMAT sticker on it. I wish they still used the Mr. Yuck sticker. And those of you who don't know what that is; look it up.

What will the new chemo regiment be? 5FU (Fluorouracil) EVERY OTHER MONDAY for 46 hrs.

Everyone other Monday we will make the drive to Duke for labs, doctor appointment, and then infusion hook up. Two hours after the pump hook up, we will go home with the chemo for 46 hours. A nurse will disconnect Tony from his pump on Wednesdays.

Needless to say, Mondays are going to be looooooooooong days. I don't know how he does it. How in the world does he find the strength? Then again, people ask me every day, how the Hell do I do it – you know – with the kids, and the job, and the hubby, and the in-laws. My answer is simple.

I just do it.

Tony always says, "Too easy," like the doctor told him to take two aspirin and call him in the morning.

I sat Alec and Austin down this morning and broke the news of how it's going to be for the rest of our lives, at least for the next few months. I reminded them that their job is NOT TO BE STRONG.

That is MY job.

Their job is to be a son. To do well in school.

Austin, "It's your senior year of high school. It's SAT and College Apps, or I'm dragging your butt to the Army Recruiting Station and pushing you on the Army bus," I say with love of course.

I asked them to help me keep Aydin and Ashton out of my bed during the chemo days. We can't have any oops-es with Mr. Yuck here and the boys. Otherwise, I expect them to continue to be a team with me. Life will have to continue as it did six years ago.

Football is still on Fridays and Saturdays.

I still have to go to work Monday through Friday.

My children still get bumps and bruises and the lawn still has to be mowed, dinner made, and so on. I just would like it done without the bickering so Dad can rest and maybe we can all save each other some sanity.

Finally, one of the boys blurted out today that his father is dying and no one understands what WE are going through. As much as I HATED hearing it, I'm glad this one in particular is opening up. Another one has been having nightmares about Tony dying and waking up in the middle of the night sweaty as Hell. And I had a horrible nightmare last night about Tony's last breath.

I HATE THIS.

Tony is actually looking amazing these past two days but that fear still haunts my home and my kids. I have to bring normalcy back into my household. I have to let the boys get away for a few days to enjoy life and THAT IS OK. So, they all went away this weekend to a friend's, or family's house.

Me, where's my break?

I don't get one. I don't want one. I just want to lay in bed, curled up with my husband and enjoy the sound of nothing. That's as much break as I need.

None Of Us Are Promised Tomorrow

Wednesday, August 16, 2017

What would you do differently if someone told you, you only had six months to live?

Makes you think right?

Would you still get mad? Would you cry? Would you go skydiving? What would you do? What would you not do. What would you stop doing?

Well what if you were told your loved one only had six months of life left?

Now what would you do differently? Do you tell other people? Do you get angry? Do you kiss your love one?

The truth is, when you do tell people, the words, "DON'T GIVE UP HOPE," always come to light!! It's OK. for me to continue to watch Tony suffer and in pain as long as I don't give up hope. Is that right? Is that what you're telling me?

When you don't tell people, you hold the stress inside yourself like a poisen. Everyone asks you, "what's wrong?" all the time.

The truth is, none of us know what we will do until someone shares that information with us. And, if you are anything like the rest of us you cry and get angry. And the worst part? You start shutting your loved one out; start closing the door that separates "our life" from "my life" and "your life."

Have I been told Tony has only six months?

No I have not. Please let me make that clear. Is there a prognosis? OF COURSE there is. But, I chose to share that with a few select people that WANT to know.

WHY? Because my childrens' feelings matter.

WHY ELSE? Because if you TRULY cared about my Tony, then your butt would've been spending time with him all this time not just when time is getting short.

SHOCKING I say that, right? But its true. We are human. We have busy lives. And, we get so caught up in our own lives that it's easy to forget about our dear friends and what they may be going through.

Does it make you a bad person? HELL NO!!!

Does it mean I don't love you? OF COURSE NOT.

But, I personally cannot keep continuing to want for other people. It's just too hard.

NONE OF US ARE PROMISED TOMORROW.

So if you are standing in front of someone you love, TELL THEM.

If you want to eat that piece of apple pie, EAT IT.

If you want to go to Figi, GO!!

Stop making excuses and enjoy life and make memories.

Tony and I have decided it's time to make memories. I already have regrets of not enjoying more good times with my brother before he died. I refuse to let the boys and me have the same kind of regrets. Tony keeps telling me, It's going to be OK. But, I am so scared it's not going to be.

While Tony is hooked up to his 5FU pump, he is so active and making me coffee in the morning, etc. It's when the pump is disconnected that he's so sick. He looks so pale during chemo. But then he says he feels the best he's felt in a long time. So, I guess the chemo is working.

With that said, I'll end on this.

Last week, I received an amazing opportunity when I was asked to speak at the National Institute of Health (NIH) National Institute of Nursing Research (NINR) Caregiver Summit.

For those that don't know, the NIH is the primary agency of the United States government responsible for biomedical and public health research. It's mandate includes the National Cancer Institute, and much more. Speaking at the NINR Summit was surreal. I can't even begin to tell you what a dream come true it was. Being able to share my story and offer some experience, strength, and hope to others in my shoes was remarkable.

I love speaking and helping others.

The other day I received an email from *Cancer Today* magazine asking me for an interview for an article they are writing in their Winter issue.

Talk about blown away!

You see, I love that I can give back, but I HATE that I my husband and kids are enduring this journey which gives me these opportunities. For anyone who'd like to see me speak, you may at NIH NINR Caregiver Summit Day 1 on YouTube© Our panel begins at 1:03:30, and I am the second speaker at 1:25:00.

I learned so much at this summit and met some great people!!

Never give up on your dreams. No one is promised tomorrow. If you were told you had six months to live, do what you would do NOW!!!

End Of The Road

What does it mean when we come to the end of the road?

What does it mean when we hear, "Just take me home."

At what point do we let our loved one rest?

When do we say enough is enough?

My dear friend is coming to the end of her journey. It hurts, making me deeply sad. I think about her boys and her husband. I think about the urinals she collects and has all over her bathroom. Her smile just lights up a room. But I know she is so tired. She is holding on for all of us and at WHAT TIME do we say, "I love you and its OK. Well be alright. Your kids will make it just fine, grow up, live happy lives and never forget you?"

Our first instinct is to call every major cancer institute and book the first flight to the nearest clinical trial location. We get on the computer and we research the latest drugs, when what we really should be doing is lying next to our loved one and holding them tight.

Then the guilt.

Did I try hard enough?

What if that drug worked?

Will we ever know? Oh the guilt.

What most people on the outside the cancer circle don't know is that when it's time, the person we are fighting for, the person we love, won't be the same person anymore. Their journey will have taken too much of a toll on them. The words we share aren't whispers of love like it was.

Sometimes, for about five seconds in the middle of the night, you may share that old love, but when your head hits the pillow, your eyes close and you dream of how love used to be, and hope that when you wakeup you'll discover that it was the cancer that was the dream – a very, very, terrible dream.

The truth is, letting your loved one rest may be easier than watching them go through more pain and poking and prodding just to selfishly allow us one more month, or two more weeks with them on earth.

I say all this with tears pouring down my face because one day, I will be the one making that decision for Tony. When is enough enough? How do we Know we have really come to the end of that final road? There comes a time in our lives when we have to say goodbye. It's never when we want to, it's when it's time for our loved ones to go.

They get tired. They are worn out – physically, emotionally, spiritually – but trust me, they are saying, "Please remember us how we once were. Remember the good times, remember the laughs, remember the stories, and smiles, for we aren't far away, just a memory. For now it is time for God to wrap his arms around me and bring me home."

Not The Answers We Wanted

Tuesday, October 03, 2017

I'm sitting here typing trying to figure out how to share the news that I was told on Friday. It's news that made me cry, news that made me scared. But, it's also news that motivated me.

A month ago Tony started throwing up multiple times a day. He can't keep any food down. I had no idea it had gotten so bad until I came home from a football game and he told me he had thrown up 12 times while I was gone. I also noticed a couple of days later enemas appeared in the trash can. Tony went from diarrhea to constipated in a very short time.

He had kept that part from me.

No med changes. Same chemo. But, now, new symptoms. I had noticed Tony's pain had returned and I began to worry.

We shared this information when we went to chemo and they ordered emergency CT of his abdomen and pelvis, only to learn there was NOTHING wrong; at least that they could see. So we went upstairs for his 5FU chemo and went home.

This round was odd.

The vomiting was worse and Tony started vomiting only through his nose in his sleep. I tell you this not to make you sick, but to maybe help another person one day. I emailed his doctor immediately. When we went to Duke last week and finished up scans with chest and head.

RESULTS: Aspiration in lungs has increased. He's throwing up so much it's now collecting in his lungs. And then I saw it.

I was reading the CT results to see, "Distal Esophageal Wall Thickening." In the cancer world, thickening is NOT a word you want to see. I immediately emailed the doc again.

I fought back tears the whole drive home. I knew something was wrong and started stomping my feet. I demanded an endoscopy and ASAP. We got a barium swallow study only to learn that Tony has a narrowing in his esophagus where the cancer was the first time. I sent the results to his doctors and asked his oncologist to call me. We had a great conversation and, just as I had suspected, based on symptoms, the swallow study, and CT scan, the current chemotherapy is not working.

Keeping that news from Tony was harder than ever. It was fear, anger, frustration and fighting for the man I love with every drop of blood I have, battling so hard, but it doesn't seem to be doing a bit of good. He's just laying there clueless as to what is growing inside of him. I finally broke down yesterday and told him.

"What's wrong baby?" He asked. "I know you are keeping something from me."

"I don't know how to tell you," I answer, beganing to cry.

"I think I already know," he answered.

"I don't think the chemo is working baby." I whisper. "We are having to add another drug to the next round."

Tony tried to hide them, but I felt his tears drip on my arm as he buried his face. He said, "It's not fair," quickly followed by, "OK, I'll do whatever I have to do." He's such a trooper, but I fear that this treatment will be too hard on him. It's similar to what he had five years ago. This time, Oxaliplatin is the chemo they're adding.

Then I question why are we doing this?

Will this even work?

What kind of wife would want the love of her life to go through this?

Then I remember—he wants to fight. He is not ready to give up and I have to support him either way.

It wasn't easy telling the older boys the chemo wasn't working. I practiced on a couple of family members so that I wouldn't be a blubbering fool. When it comes to Tony's health, the boys sort of take their lead from me. If I'm worried or crying, they do the same. I have to stay positive; and so do they.

THE RAW PART

How the hell am I supposed to stay positive? It's hard when all my friends' husbands, wives, and dads are entering or are in Hospice.

I'm sitting here every night kissing my love before bed wondering if that will be the last time.

I ask myself, if all this pain he is in is only going to give me a few more weeks, WHY? WHY DO THIS TO HIM? I want a CURE not a treatment. Let's try this. Let's try that. And, when we fall, we just keep getting back up. THAT'S WHY because maybe, just maybe, on one of those tries we won't fall. We will have success.

I PRAY!!

Now the plan is scope next week, followed by 5FU and Oxaliplatin chemotherapy. Nothing cold for Tony moving forward.

I'll tell you what was NOT in the plan though, Tony breaking his thumb and needing a cast.

SERIOUSLY!!

If cancer isn't enough, now we have to break bones.

In the meantime, I will love on my hubby, give him extra kisses, and snuggle with him every chance I get it, don't ever forget WHY you're fighting. It's the relationship we treasure.

I'm fighting for the love of my life.

The Struggle Is Real...
And So Is His Pain

Monday, November 13, 2017

There is a part of caregiving no one likes to talk about. The guilt part.

It finds you when the doctor reduces or increases chemo.

It finds you when treatment decisions need to be made and you always seem to choose what WE think will save our loved one's life when, in fact, it just may be speeding up the inevitable.

What if the decision was wrong?

What if the best choice was to just do nothing and have faith that God will heal or allow you to enjoy your life without having to deal with poison to flow through your veins?

This is a struggle I deal with with Tony every other week. The last three rounds of chemo have all been different. Round Four: normal 5FU. Round Five: 5FU + Oxaliplatin (FOLFOX). Round Six: FOLFOX with a 40 percent reduction in 5FU chemo because of the side effects and newly emerging heart issues.

Two weeks ago I found myself calling 911 because Tony was having chest pains and I ran into our bedroom and threw my ear on his chest.

His heart was out of sync and beating all funny. Of course I was scared until EMS showed up and in turned out he was perfectly fine.

Go figure right?

I was ready to scream because here we are again with symptoms with no documentation, or evidence of anything pointing to proper treatment. Of course, they couldn't find anything at the hospital, and so we just went home.

The next few days Tony had increased pain and it seemed as though his meds didn't work at all. So, we would dope him up by giving him an ativan to knock him out so he could sleep through it.

Don't judge until you are going through it. It's not easy watching your loved one in so much pain. You'd rather just watch them sleep.

Like when your hellacious three year old finally falls asleep after a long, hard, trying-your-patience kind of day. You walk in to check on them and they are sound asleep like the most innocent angel. Trust me when I say, it's the same with Tony.

My struggles are real and only God can judge me.

I think about life if Tony completes his journey and immediately feel guilty for even thinking it. I worry about my children after their daddy is gone and I get angry when people tell me, I'm young, and strong, and will find a way to move on. Don't tell me that when I am loving my warrior through it. Instead please just come do my laundry or hold me when I cry.

No words will comfort me right now, for I am scared like everyone else, I'm just not allowed to show it.

When Daddy Dies

Thursday, November 16, 2017

I saw him lying there on the floor.

He looked as if he was just sleeping.

Could this be real?

Why did this happen?

Did he just lay down his life for his son?

Tony's daddy struggled with Tony's cancer diagnosis, especially the recurrence. I remember him in the hospital ICU back in June, me begging the doctors NOT to make me choose between my father-in-law and my husband. I was caring for both of them. Tony had not started chemo at the time and Robert needed my undivided attention. He was finally on track with his medicine and doing so well...and then Tony started chemo.

It is as if his heart could not handle it.

He buried his pain and tried to hide it from all of us. But, he didn't have me fooled. We made a pact to stay healthy. We had to be strong for our spouses. We had to be strong for Tony.

It was Austin's Senior Night and, of course, we were running late. Robert called and I had missed his call. He had called Tony at 7:41pm that night telling him he had a hard time breathing. Tony told him to call 911 because we were at Austin's football game. We immediatly started packing up to head to him. Tony's mom called Tony and said Robert had passed out on the floor. This time I called 911 but they were already in route. When EMS got there, he was gone. A massive heart attack in combination with COPD. And, I'd say, maybe even a broken heart.

Tony's mom was also not doing well. Her vitals were all over the place. "PLEASE," Tony begged, "Take my mom to the hospital. I can't lose both of my parents tonight."

While Tony's mom was in the hospital I did the hardest thing of all and asked for help. All hands on deck. I had to get their house cleaned. It took a whole day and then some, but with the help of family and friends, we got it done.

Tony's mom came home to our house. She didn't want to see anyone while she was in the hospital, but now people were coming over to see her and Tony. We finalized a few things with the funeral and took her to get her hair done and pedicure.

ANYTHING to make her feel a little better about herself.

Someone in my position, a caregiver to a cancer patient, has thought about being left behind. Being a widow/widower. I thought about someone trying to tell me what I could or could not do if something happened to Tony. AND trust me, I DARE THEM. I DARE someone to tell my mother-in-law she can't eat a piece of candy or smoke a cigarette. She just lost her husband of 46 years. Give her a break!!

Robert Leonard passed away suddenly and painlessly. But he left a legacy, and one that he should be proud of. He left beautiful land, and a place to fish. He left a wealth of knowledge and stories of strength and courage. He was a HERO and a PROTECTOR. He was buried with full Military Honors. The folded flag was presented to Tony's mom with tears pouring down our faces.

Tony collapsed on his father's casket while my youngest Ashton broke down and cried so hard and loud. I can't imagine what its like to lose a parent. I still have mine. I still can pick up the phone and call mine and say, "I love you."

The whole time while I watched my boys cry over their Papa I couldn't help but anticipate what it will be like for them when Daddy Dies. Whether it's a month from now, or a year, or a decade, one day it will happen. I don't care what they say, all the boys, all five of them, are daddy's boys. Just like Tony and Jeff, were daddy's boys.

Tony's strength through all of this has been extremely inspirational. He is just so strong and upbeat right now. He's making the hard days a lot easier. He has his moments, but his daddy wouldn't want him to cry and be sad. As we say in our house, death isn't always sad, being in heaven with God is a gift!!

I'll miss you papa in law.

I'll always think about you.

I'll always keep your stories alive.

I'll always keep this family together.

I'll love you forever.

xoxo

Your Daughter-In-Law

His Bucket List

Saturday, December 02, 2017

After Tony's cancer went in remission, I made him a promise. I promised him that if his cancer ever came back we would make memories and I would make sure his bucket list happened.

Let's face it we can do one of two things when we get diagnosed with a terminal illness. One, we can mope and cry and whine and be depressed about it, or two, we can live life.

None of us are truly promised tomorrow. So I did what I think any spouse would do in my situation. I got some money together, cringing at the thought knowing that I'd have less for the future, and I started making all of Tony's dreams come true.

~ He always wanted his three car garage: Check

~ He always wanted an upgraded kitchen: Check

~ He always wanted to go on a cruise: Check

~ He always likes UNC Duke basketball games: Check

~ He wanted matching tattoos: Check

I also promised my boys that I would plan the trip of a lifetime. Making a memory with their daddy and take lots of pictures, so I did. Seven days in the Eastern Caribbean on the largest ship in the world. I booked the trip in September and dared anyone to give me a hard time about taking the kids out of school.

When Tony's daddy died unexpectedly I realized how short life really is. I watched his mom cry and put her head down, not wanting to eat, and all I could think was, is this what it will be like for me?

I told him yesterday that you better add some things to your bucket list, because my biggest fear is that February 8th when we go to the basketball game, his list will be complete. But there is so much more life to live and participate in.

I think what hurt me, is that someone accused us of using money from Tonys dad's passing to do all this.

It makes me sick that I'm trying to make my husband's dreams come true so he can enjoy it and people want to hate and accuse.

Don't you people get it?

Don't you know I would trade *anything* to have Tony be cancer-free, to not be sick, to not need medications every five minutes?

I don't want your money people. I want your love and support. I want your friendship. I want you to come visit and spend time with us. You can't catch cancer. Don't judge me, don't assume, *ask*.

I am making his dreams come true and, trust me when I say, I'm crying through it. You can choose to do one of two things when you are diagnosed with a terminal illness.

We are choosing to live.

A Love Lost - Debbie Zelman

For the first time in a really long time I have no words. I don't have the right thing to say. I have no words of encouragement, only words of pain and sadness. I know she would *never* want me to dwell on her loss.

She would want me to turn that pain and anger and frustration into motivation.

She would want me to lift her family up in prayer and encourage her children to finish school and carry on in her legacy.

She told me a funny story about how her husband Andy went to work in scrubs one day instead of a suit and she was caught off guard. She has shared with me how our children are so much alike because all they have ever known is cancer.

They didn't know mom and dad before cancer. Sarah was three, like Aydin was four. We talked about teenagers and college applications. We talked about boyfriends and girl friends of those teenagers, and oh the similarities. We talked about being neighbors and how we would never sleep. Our friendship was more than just stomach cancer. Stomach cancer truly was our passion. It's what brought us together. But our families were our hearts and souls.

Debbie Zelman was like a sister to me.

I would never say she was my sister because I would never take that bond from her true beautiful sisters, the ones she played hopscotch and Barbies with. But she inspired me. She mentored me. She empowered me to not sit on my butt and allow doctors to have the final say in Tony's care. She taught me how to be a voice. And, though her voice won't be on the other end when I call, her message will continue to be shouted from the rooftops.

We shared tears and, "F bombs," when appropriate. We shared laughter and frustration.

Today I woke up with puffy eyes, for my dear friend is soaring with the angels. I have a lump in my throat that won't go away. I have a pain in my chest that makes it hard to breath. She and Tony encouraged each other to keep fighting the fight. To me, my friend was invincible.

But like we all know, cancer has no remorse. I am scared. I am sad. I am broken hearted.

I was crying at my desk yesterday and Ashton crawled into my lap. I told him, "Not now," and tried to push him off. Instead he wrapped his arms around my neck and held on tight and said, "It's OK. Mommy." I couldn't help but latch on and just cry. I cried so hard.

My baby, my seven year old, did to me what I do to him when he is sad, angry, and scared. He forced me to let it out. He said its not fair that everyone is dying. And I said, "No baby, it's not." I have to believe and have faith that God really does have a plan. I have to believe that there is a special place in heaven for our warriors.

Every time I stop and take a deep breath, I can see Debbie's smile. I can hear her telling me it's going to be OK. She is telling me to keep the torch lit and to not let her dream be silenced. She's telling me that she's always going to be looking over us. Debbie's smile could light up a room. But Debbie was tired. She didn't want us to remember her that way. She would want us to use her death as a stepping stone in carrying her message. That is what Debbie would want. Any angle to find a cure for this horrible disease.

So my dear friend, I made you a promise that I WILL KEEP!!! I will keep advocating and fighting for a cure. I will continue to raise awareness and I will continue to keep your legacy alive. I miss you and I love you. A love was lost, but I PROMISE YOU will NEVER be forgotten.

How About Some Good News?

Is there such thing in the cancer world as good news?

Hell yeah there is!! It's called good news in life, because if you are still living in the cancer world, then its a GREAT day.

I would just have to start off with, "Thank God 2017 is over. Too many lost. Too many deaths. Too much pain and sorrow. It was about time that my family get some news that was fantastic!!

Not only did Alec, (our 21 year old) get offered a full time job with the company he was temping for, we had an amazing time on our cruise.

We finished closing out Tony's daddy's estate. By the way, if you are ever left as the executor of someone's will, I feel sorry for you, "Please dear God," I begged my parents to not leave me responsible. Obviously if it's hard work, it can't by definition be easy. Austin has really been amazing and a true rock for me. He reminded me that he doesn't focus on dad being sick. He focuses on the fact he can still do things with his dad. He is truly mature beyond his years. Alec and Austin started taking their little brothers out and spending time with them, which is something I had been praying for for a while.

They need each other. Plus, I need "Me Time." My older sister and I had a fantastic conversation today about, "Me Time," and how she wants me to schedule 30 minutes of, "Me Time," a day. Six years ago I remember telling her that I really needed her now. The truth is, she and I have reconciled now, at the perfect time in both of our lives. Even my oldest son came and joined us for New Year's dinner. It's like everything for once is falling into place.

In 2017 I never thought that anything would ever come together, or that I would ever wake from this nightmare. But, you know what? When you stop focusing on negativity, it's amazing all of the positive things that are going on that we miss.

What defines us is how we get up every morning when life continues to beat us down. It's how we set examples of strength and dignity and practicing what we preach. If I say, "Take time to smell the roses," I had sure as Hell better have some in my yard. If I say, "Spend time with the ones you love because none of us are promised tomorrow," I better be enjoying time with my family. Walk the walk, not just talk the talk.

What do I truly think is really great? Tony and I are more in love than ever. We aren't fussing at each other or the kids. We take the time to snuggle, we sneak kisses every second we get. We are so happy. Our family is finally coming together again. No shoe will drop, we are really just enjoying it.

Tony's health is going to have ups-and-downs, and right now it's up. His scans are stable. He's finding a balance with both his chemo and this crazy thing called life.

It feels good to take a deep breath and have time to feel the exhale actually leave my lungs. We both lost a lot of friends and family these past three months. Not only did Debbie pass, but that same day, my Uncle Martin gained his wings leaving his esophageal cancer behind.

December was a rough month, but Tony and I realized that we need each other more than ever. Don't sweat the small stuff cause it's all small stuff. I told my boys if they do the right thing, they can't go wrong, even if it's not always accepted. You are the one who has to face yourself in the mirror each morning. I sing loud on the highway and enjoy it. What I'm really trying to say is that even though in the cancer world there are a whole lot of downs, it's OK. to smile and laugh and have great days. It's okay to celebrate the normal milestones that your children achieve. And, we should all live each day as if it's our last.

Tonight I took time and tucked my children into bed, kissed them on the cheek, and tucked the covers under their sweet chins. And I loved every minute of it. I listen to my mother-in-law when she says it all goes so fast.

Life, Love, Marriage....Enjoy them!!!

So with that, I'm going to sign off and go spend time with Tony.

If you have time, I was truly honored to be interviewed by Cancer Today Magazine about care-giving. My hats off to all caregivers! Its not easy! The interview can be found at: http://www.cancertodaymag.org/Winter2017/Pages/A-Call-toCare.aspx

I Spoke To Soon

Friday, January 12, 2018

Don't you hate it when you jinx yourself? When you say, "Thank God it's Friday," and then your work load causes you to work late? Or, you forget to knock on wood? Or, in my case, you blog about how great things are going only to be woken up five hours later to your hubby panting, "My chest hurts."

Wednesday morning at 5:00 a.m. Tony was complaining that his chest hurt. He kept mumbling over and over and over again, "My chest hurts. My chest hurts," so often it woke me up out of a dead sleep. Well, let's face it, Tony's chest always hurts.

Food gets stuck. Bile comes up the esophagus. All sorts of things. But this time something was different. Tony wasn't acting right. He wasn't answering my questions. He just said, "My chest hurts," over and over and over again. I put my ear on his chest and his heart was racing. I took his blood pressure and Tony's heart was beating 143 bpm. I quickly turned on the light. Tony's teeth were chattering and he was white as a ghost. I took his temperature. It was 102.7. At that moment I called 911.

The paramedics got there and did all his vitals, I gave them the speal and they hooked him up to the heart machine, confirming the rapid heart rate. They took him straight in. Aydin saw Tony being taken on the stretcher and started to cry. Aydin was sleeping on the couch because he had been throwing up the night before. I heard a small voice ask, "Mommy, is daddy going to be ok?" It was

Aydin. "Of course he is baby," I reassured him. This time though, Tony really scared me.

When I got to the hospital, they had already done a chest Xray. The doc came in and told me Tony had pneumonia. I said, with all due respect ma'am, this hospital is notorious for telling patients they have pneumonia and then sending them home with antibiotics, when in fact it wasn't pneumonia, but something else. I explained to her that he was a cancer patient and that there were some concerning scans regarding his chest about a month ago.

She assured me they would do a chest CT and get to the bottom of what was causing him to be so sick. See, not only was Tonys pulse racing, his blood pressure had begun to drop. It went from 90s/60s to 80s/50s and then 70s/40s. They increased his fluids to help with his bp. Four liters in five hours! He was on oxygen and he was really out of it.

When the chest CT came back, it confirmed the pneumonia. But, he had aspiration pneumonia. Tony had been throwing up so much that he was aspirating into his lungs. Because of the cancer, and the chemo, and now pneumonia, and his blood pressure not being stable, they admitted him. I quickly said, "We request transfer to Duke."

Problem.

Duke was not only on deferment, they had no beds. Cape Fear consulted with the oncologist and started three different antibiotics. The infectious disease doctor came in and tested for lots and lots of things only to learn that Tony had E Coli in his lungs.

Now I don't know about you, but I said, "How in the world do you get E Coli in your lungs???" Well, it comes from the GI track and aspiration. I just about fell on to the floor.

Because Tony was at Cape Fear I was able to go home at night, tuck the boys into bed, and get them off to school in the morning. I even left the hospital a little early Thursday to go to Austin's football banquet. I video called Tony so that he could see Austin get his senior award and receive the Special Forces award for special teams. This was a great honor and we are so proud of him.

Over the years Tony and I have learned that, especially with cancer, we have to make do and sometimes that means video calls, Face Time, whatever you want to call it, so that he can participate in the kid's activities.

Friday morning after I got the little ones after school Austin sent me a text telling me that he had thrown up. I went upstairs to check on him felt his forehead and said, "Oh boy." I got the thermometer and took his temperature, only to find out that he too was running a fever. I didn't hesitate. I took him to the doctor and had him tested for the flu. Of course, he tested positive. So now I have Tony coming home from the hospital with E Coli in his lungs and pneumonia, my right hand has the flu, and I'm just thinking, "Lord please help me."

I had a great conversation with Tony's oncologists who are coming up with a plan now that there was E Coli and pneumonia in the mix. Oh yeah, let's not forget household flu.

Not only did Duke double the length of anti biotic for Tony to be on, they also prescribe him two weeks worth of tamiflu just in case. Under no circumstances was I to have Austin anywhere near Tony because Tony can not afford to get the flu on top of everything else. Poor Austin has been quarantined in his room with his laptop making up homework with meds round the clock, lots of Gatorade, and Dayquil and Nyquil.

I have been bleaching and Lysoling the house keeping everyone in their rooms. Tony's doc also suggested that I take Tamiflu because I was caring for everyone and would be around both Austin and Tony. So apparently we cleaned out the pharmacy's entire supply of Tamiflu.

Needless to say this is all a lot and sometimes I wonder how in the Hell am I going to get through this. But then great friends and family do things like meal trains and order takeout Chinese and pizza, so dinner is one less thing that I have to worry about. A great friend brought over subs and chips and Sprite today which was perfect because we could munch on it when we were hungry while I finished sanitizing the house.

I know God doesn't give us more than we can handle, but he sure knows how to push the envelope.

It's good to have Tony home and I'm grateful that we are able to treat what he has with meds. But, this also means he won't be able to get chemo on Tuesday as planned. He will again have to skip a round of chemo because he was too sick. The chemo is what's keeping Tony's cancer at bay. I get scared when we start skipping it. In the meantime, I'm not goning to focus on that. I'm going to focus on getting my family healthy, and keeping myself healthy, because the second I get sick, all Hell will break loose.

I can't thank you all enough for your thoughts, prayers, donations, food deliveries, words of encouragement, and so much more over this past week. Please continue to pray for Tony's healing and that Austin gets over this flu. Though I normally don't ask for much I will ask this; February 27th, Debbie's Dream Foundation will be having our 6th Annual Advocacy Day on Capitol Hill. Ladies and gentlemen this is where the funds come for research – the true big pots of money – the research that will find a cure. We have to keep raising awareness, so I encourage you, if you are free that day and can make it to D.C. please join us in meeting with our legislatures and lobbying for stomach cancer awareness.

We have to tell Tony's story and Debbie's story, and your story. We have to tell our children's story. For their pain is just as real as ours. I encourage all of you to be a voice.

Tony's Wish Granted

UNC TARHEELS - BUCKET LIST COMPLETE
Monday, February 19, 2018

It's not everyday that any of us can have dreams come true. But I, for one, was not going to let Tony's bucket list go unfulfilled. Thanks to the Fill Your Bucket List Foundation, Tony was able to attend a UNC vs Duke basketball game. It was truly a night to remember. Not of course without the fussing and fighting of the two little ones, getting to the stadium late, or me getting pulled into a last minute conference call to make it truly a Leonard night to remember. But...we made it. We got to the hotel and it was beautifully decorated wtih UNC Tarheel gear and two signed basket balls – one from Eric Montross and the other from, none other than Roy Williams, head coach of UNC Basketball. I had never seen Tony smile so big. OK, maybe on our wedding day, (*WINK*) but, seriously, not in such a long, long time.

We got to dinner and rushed to the arena where we met Eric Montross. His hands were huge! He signed Tony's UNC hat, and met all the boys, and shook their hands. Everyone was so kind and helpful. Tony truly enjoyed every second of the game.

We even made the news. Check it out at:
https://www.youtube.com/watch?v=GOqgUxIrfg0

I think what scares me, is that was the last thing on Tony's bucket list. Everything he ever wanted to do was done. I told him, he needs to put some more stuff on there because we aren't done yet.

So what does the man tell me?

Hawaii. He wants to go to Hawaii. That would've been nice to know before we went on the cruise Mr. Leonard. So here I am planning yet another crazy vacation in paradise with the man I love. And honestly people, we should do it any way. Cancer or not.

Tony and I had a big scare in January.

I didn't think he was going to get passed this pneumonia. Hell, I wondered if he even had pneumonia. I feared it was the, "Big C," invading his lungs, masking itself as pneumonia. At one point he had absolutely no air moving in his left lung. His labs were going down and I didn't know what was next. I asked for all of you to pray. Pray with all your might. And you did. Six days later Tony miraculously had clear lungs and a clear CT.

Tony resumed chemo, but then lost nine pounds in ten days. Luckily, he gained most of it back from IV fluids and protein shakes. Right now we are just keeping on keeping on. It's crazy because sometimes I just feel like I'm waiting for the other shoe to drop. But honestly, I really need to enjoy every moment I have with Tony.

We are getting ready to head to D.C. for Debbie's Dream Foundation Advocacy Day next week. It's time to keep stomping those feet.

We have to keep making noise!

Stomach cancer has to become as known as other cancers – lung, prostate, breast, brain, etc!

I Lost Him When He Got Cancer

Tuesday, March 13, 2018

I started grieving the day Tony was diagnosed with cancer. I had started the journey and didn't even realize it. The day we heard cancer, I started no longer seeing myself growing old with him. I didn't plan a funeral, I didn't pick out a suit. I slowly watched the man I fell so deeply in love with change.

Things that used to be funny, weren't funny. Things that were important to us, suddenly weren't. And the people that we both swore would be there for us, just disappeared. See, cancer just didn't take away the man I fell in love with, it tested my vows. It tested friendships. It tested my faith. And, along our journey, it showed me how to fall even more deeply in love with Tony.

It's easy to get so frustrated and angry. "Why are you buying sports stuff Tony?"

"Really, *another* watch?"

"When the Hell did you get this into guns?"

"How are you too sick for this, but not too sick for that?"

That is the grief talking.

The reason I find myself so upset and angry with Tony sometimes is because I lost the man I fell in love with. You see, the man I fell in love with didn't buy stupid stuff. He didn't collect guns. And, he was so energetic he never missed a single ball practice.

The man I fell in love with hardly took Tylenol and now injects enough narcotics to kill a herd of cows. The tiniest light at night drove him nuts, and now all lights and TV's must be on. He was never a sleepwalker. He never got upset. He always smiled. And he always took me out.

Cancer introduced me to a whole new man.

A man that has more strength than someone who can bench 700 lbs. A man that reminds me that dates and going out are special, and not expected. A man with passion that has to still smile when all he wants to do is cry and ask, "Why me?" I see a man that fought a battle harder than any solider in a war because let's face it, there is no R&R in this war, and there is no heroic return home. Instead it's, "Do I get to live to see another day doc?" I fell in love with a new man that stole my heart faster than he did before.

For ten years, I have stood by and seen Tony bury a brother, a brother-in-law, his daddy. He's fought to keep his family together, fought cancer, and now he's watching his mother slowly die of a broken heart – all while continuing to be a good father, a loving husband, and a supportive son. Now I'm sorry if that isn't good enough for some people, but I am so grateful I lost the man I fell in love with and now have this *amazing* man changed by cancer. Tony is *exceptional.*

Cancer changed me too.

It has taught me enough organization skills that I can run ten countries single handily. I've learned how to ask for help, I've learned who I can count on, and how to set up boundaries. I've learned patience, and wisdom, caring, and being kind. I've learned what unconditional love is. I've learned how to love him through it. I've learned about *living*.

Spouses get it when we say it's been a long journey, but we didn't lose them when they died. We lost them when they were diagnosed. Very few truly understand what it means. But the other side of the coin is, we also fell in love all over again with someone new. Someone that was stronger than our first love. Our warriors learn to be more appreciative. They tend to be more sensitive. And, they tend to be more understanding.

Now that's on a good day, because on the bad days, Lord we are grieving that first love and miss them oh so much. That's why we are sad and angry, because we are grieving life before cancer. And that's OK because our warriors do it too.

It hurts.

It sucks.

It's painful.

I'm tired.

I don't know how I do it, so please don't ask. I don't have a choice, and neither does Tony. There is no alternative for us. Instead, please just come over and help. Be a friend. I am so tired, I don't know which way is up or down. I can't thank our friends enough who are there. We love you dearly. Tonight though, I'm grieving my old life. I'm stressed today. I'm tired of crying today. Today was a hard day for me.

So, tonight before you all go to bed, look at the person you love. Embrace them. Love them. Tell them how much you care about them. Beause there are lots of spouses out their grieving a loss. That can't have those conversations anymore. They just want to be loved how they once were. There is a father who just wants his sons to love him regardless. I pray that our boys see that Tony is leading by example. Getting up and fighting every day – for *them*. I pray that my younger boys continue to see their daddy as a hero. I pray for peace for his mother. Finally, I pray for those that judge my family and are causing us pain. I thank those who are there for us bringing us joy, and meals, and company, always.

Not Her Too

Something's not right. I can feel it. My mother in law hadn't been the same since Robert passed, and frankly who would be? She struggled with congestive heart failure, diabetes, and high blood pressure...all can be treated with medication. But what can't be, is a broken heart. She entered hospice six weeks ago. Her heart was functioning only at 20%. It was a difficult decision, but the help she received was amazing. She had an aide, a nurse, pastor, and best part, no more hospitals.

It was the begining of Spring Break. Tony needed some much father-son time with the boys, I needed a break, and Cindy wanted some freedom. So we scheduled 5 days of respite care during Spring Break. It was Easter weekend. I'll never forget. Cindy came to the table as the boys were going through their Easter baskets. She asked me for her checkbook. "No Cindy. You don't need your checkbook." I told her. My mother in law didn't take no very well, so after she insisted I got it. She wrote each of the boys a check for $50.00 for Easter. Then she started writing a letter in Korean. When she was done, she slowly walked back to her room. After a short minute, she called for me. I checked her vitals. Her heart was racing, and her blood pressure was through the roof. I gave her her blood pressure meds and layed with her in her bed.

Austin took the boys over to his moms house for Easter dinner. We were invited, but I couldn't leave Cindy. While I layed with her she placed her hand onto my cheek. She said, "You're the best." I began to cry. Something wasn't right.

That night around 4am, I heard a cry from the living room. It was Cindy and she was lying on the floor. I helped her up and we walked back to her room. She put her hands on the door frame as to stop from going in. "Robert, Mommy. Robert, Mommy." She called. As she called out to her husband and mother, I broke down. I got her settled in the bed, and called the on call nurse. When they got there, she was stable. "Something's not right, I'M TELLING YOU!" I insisted. "I'll have your regular nurse come see her later today," she responded.

Her aide came by, but her nurse was on vacation that week. Her aide knew her well. She tried to give her a bath, but Cindy wasn't having it. She just wanted to rest. Cindy's breathing was labored, and something was just off. She continued to ask me when she was going to "the place," referring to respite care at SECU Hospice House. "Tomorrow," I'd tell her.

Tony spent the evening with his mom. Tony's best friend came over and sat with both of them. The sight was beautiful, yet painful. A sick son, siting with his sick mother.

The next morning, Cindy asked me for a strawberry milkshake. If there is anything I've learned at this point, you get what you want Mrs. Leonard. She asked me to give her a bath, and so I did. She wanted to look nice for her mini vacation. She was weak. Her oxygen was at 4 liters. The younger boys hugged her good bye and went upstairs to pack. She asked me to read the bible to her, and so I did.

Tony and Austin drove her to what I thought was her 5 day mini vacation at respite care, instead she was admitted. The fluid in her lungs had been building, and no medication was helping. The pain in her back and chest had been building from the pressure. She was dying, and I didn't even know.

Just as I closed my eyes that same night, I received a phone call from SECU. "You need to come," they said. I tried to wake up Tony, but he had already taken his meds and was out of it. I left him a note and sped to Smithfield, about 45 min away. When I got there, her room was cold, and she had only a sheet. The women who was always cold, was now hot. I stayed all night and spoke with the team in the morning.

"She's transitioning Christy."

"WHAT DOES THAT MEAN?" I demanded answers. They handed me a pamphlet and explained the phases of dying. The staff was kind, and accomidating. It didn't make sense.

Cindy woke for a brief minute. She reached out to me and I hugged her and told her I loved her so much. I stepped outside and called Tony. He didn't want to believe it. He put on his poker face and him and Austin drove up. When Tony arrived, Cindy opened her eyes and smiled. She was so happy to see her baby boy. He came. No words were spoken, but everything was said at that moment.

She was no longer responding. All the boys came up and said their goodbyes. Five short months ago, these boys said goodbye to their Papa, and now their Grandma.

It was 10:00 at night. Cindys breathing began to change. Tony looked at me and said, "I can't do this." "Yes you can baby." I assured him. I pressed the nurses button. Tony holding her right hand, I her left. "What do I do?" I asked the nurse. "Talk her to Heaven." She said.

"Go find Robert, Cindy. Its okay. Jeff will be there too. We will be okay." I told her with tears pouring down my face. Just then, it was quiet. I looked over at Tony, and he broke down. First his bro bro, then his pops, now his mama. All I could do was hold him.

After a few minutes, I knew I had to be the one to make the phone calls. I called Anthoney and Alec, but Austin, Aydin, and Ashton were at SECU with us. Another unjustifiable phone call to share with my boys.

Myong (Cindy) Leonard, 69, of Fayetteville, passed away Wednesday evening, April 4, 2018 with her son Tony and his wife Christy by her side.

She was born on July 21, 1948 in South Korea. She was the successful business owner of Boone Trail Barbershop for over 15 years. Nothing gave her more joy than having her family together. To many she was a second mother with a heart of gold always ensuring you were warm, and had something to eat, while receiving great advice.

No more medicine or pain or hospital stays
Dear Mama Leonard gained her wings yesterday
Fiesty and stubborn with a heart of gold
She truly had a beautiful soul
We guided you to heaven and with no fear of death
Our hands were all joined as you took your last breath
You fought the good fight, you have finished the race

You have kept the faith...with dignity and grace
Fly with the angels Mama Leonard, we will always love you

Cancer Is Tearing My Family Apart

Wednesday, May 02, 2018

Weddings. Funerals. Graduations. Birthdays.

These are the occasions that bring us together. We share memories, laughter, candles, cake. We celebrate a milestone. Yes at death, many people celebrate, so don't be all shocked because I included funeral. If you dress up, it's a special occasion.

But who dresses up when you go to the oncologist, or the hospital for chemo? Who picks out their favorite outfit to sit their kids or parent down to say, I have cancer? Not *one single, solitary, person*. And if you do, you are lying to yourself. I don't know one person that wears their Sunday best to an eight hour poking and prodding chemo session. When was the last time you were in a chemo ward ladies and gentleman? Its not full of cheer or song. Trust me. The videos on YouTube© are one in a gazillion.

When I sat down and told my kids that Tony's cancer was back, one latched on to me, one latched on to Tony, one ran upstairs, one put his hands in his face, and the oldest wasn't there...but found out somehow and called me upset.

Five different reactions, all to the same news. There were no celebrations, memories, laughter, or milestones. It was fear, anger, sadness, and defeat. After a five year cancer free anniversary, we *all* had to go through it – again.

The #TEAMTONY page was created. The FoodTrain© was started. T-Shirt orders and donations came pouring in. All greatly appreciated and needed, because Lord knows gas isn't cheap and neither are medical bills.

The support we received in the beginning was nothing short of amazing. We put on this good front, but what was happening behind closed doors was the complete opposite. Cancer was tearing my family apart.

One was getting angry. In his eyes, Tony could do no wrong and I was always the bad guy.

The next one now understanding that daddy would have cancer forever broke his heart. His life ruined because his daddy cannot do with him all that his older brothers were able to enjoy.

Another child, grades suffering because his family was put first. His priority was what *we* needed. Making sacrifices for his family was more important than school.

Another son, isn't emotionally capable of watching Tony battle it again, so he runs. He feels lost, like no one understands what he is going through. He feels alone because truly, deep down, he doesn't want to disappoint his dad and he feels like he's done just that.

Finally the last one, not knowing where he fits, where he can help, or even if he's accepted? These feelings they all have that *no one, no one* understands. Not me. Not Tony. Not their friends. Instead of them leaning on each other, they resent it.

And then, there is Tony.

Tony does not care. He just wants his children to spend time with him, and help him. But he can't get that from everyone. And he gets angry. He wants so much to teach them how to do things. Oh and when the boys say, "You would think he would feel this or would say that." Let me tell you son, you don't know what he is feeling so how *dare* you mention that. Or, people on the outside say, "Tony needs to do this or do that." What he *needs* to do is fight for his life.

Finally, there is me.

How is this woman keeping it all together? Coffee, writing, deep breaths, and boundaries. I scream and ask for help. Sometimes I get it, and sometimes I don't. I don't risk my blessings by wishing anything negative on anyone. Unfortunately, this journey has taught me to remove the filter over my mouth and say how I really feel – good and bad. And I've learned that sometimes your best support comes from the strangers that send you an email to say they are praying for you. Or the boss who says, "Take the rest of the day off and do what you need to do." Or the friend that cheers on your son at Field Day because you can't be there and gives them a Capri Sun saying, "It's from your mom." It's the lady you met on the train who calls you out of the blue to say, "Something told me to call you today," or the best friends who have karaoke night while hanging insulation at 1:00 a.m. just to see you smile. Or the girl friend who shows up with pizza so you don't have to cook.

But the truth is y'all. My family is hurting.

My husband is in pain and has anger in his heart that I don't have the strength or power to remove. He is hurt. He doesn't feel like the man he used to be – and, let's face it, none of us allow him to be – out of fear. It doesn't help that he lost his brother on Nov 1, 2009, or that on Oct 27, 2017 he lost his daddy, and five months later, Apr 4, 2018, we talked his mom to heaven. Tony has outlived every member of his immediate family all while beating one of the deadliest cancers.

God has a message for him. A message of hope and faith. However, he feels all alone. We have to all pray for him that he finds it. We are a family that I have worked hard to blend, but cancer is breaking us. And at the end of the day, Tony isn't the one that is going to have to live with regret, or pain, or guilt when he gains his wings. It's us. It's his child that didn't pick up the phone to call, his friend that never came to see him, or the stranger that judged him.

When someone gets ill or dies, everyone is there in the beginning, but it's those that stay along for the journey that mean the most. I encourage everyone who reads this today; do something nice for a family that is having a hard time. Maybe mow their grass. Don't ask, Just do it. Offer to do laundry. Take the kids for the weekend or the afternoon. Bring them a meal, it doesn't have to be fancy. Offer your elbow grease. Or show up with a bottle of wine (alcohol free for me). Just be there for one another, and don't expect *anything* in return.

...And Now We Wait...
Heavy Heart & Tears

Today was a long day.

Not only were we running late, of course, due to traffic on 95 and 40, today was scan day. Scans that were supposed to be May 21, were now today, May 7. Tony hasn't been getting full chemo treatments because he hasn't been well enough. Between high white blood cell counts, infections, and more, our dear warrior has received only one dose of one of his two chemo drugs in the past six weeks.

In March, his CT showed a possible infection in his lungs. Antibiotics were prescribed, but Tony was still coughing in his sleep and running low grade fevers. Nothing seemed to get him better. But, he really wasn't any worse either. His mental state has been kind of blah. The doctors and I chalked that up to the fact that he's still grieving the loss of his mom.

I mean shoot, who wouldn't be right?

My stomach had been in knots all day and really since the end of January when the pneumonia and other junk in his lungs started. Last week's chest Xray didn't tell us much except that he didn't have pneumonia. It was something else but nobody seemed to know exactly what.

CT scan today showed the spot on his lung from March, that was thought to be an "infection," was now more solid and had doubled in size. Unclear metastasis the CT says.

Can't confirm or deny.

The question? Does it matter when it comes to a Stage IV patient and course of treatment? Honestly, not really. Either watch it and see how he does over the next couple of months, biopsy it, and move on to the third line harsher chemo that he still has to save his strength up for, or what?

What exactly *is* the plan? Why don't you have the answer? But, honestly, we don't know until we consult with the pulmonary team.

Tony's cancer is nearly impossible to detect on scans but, Dear God in Heaven, we have to know something. Nevertheless, there was no reason for Tony to continue his current chemo over the next few weeks, especially if its not working. He needs time to heal and regain his strength.

The Family: the older boys know and we have decided to wait until after Austin's graduation to rescan and test to see what that spot is doing. The younger boys are just excited that daddy gets a break in chemo and going to Duke.

Me? I'm a damn mess, but I have to stay strong when, truly y'all, I just want to cry and crawl into bed and cuddle up with Tony and forget about the world.

Our 11th year wedding anniversary is coming up. I think I'll just lay in bed with hubby all day. I just don't think any of this is fair and my family really could use a break right now.

Tony?

He's been awfully quiet. He doesn't really like to know what's going on with his body or what's wrong, just how we can fix it. He's not thrilled about the break in chemo because of what we have seen in the past. He's still grieving the loss of his parents while fighting for his life. I can't even imagine y'all. I can't. All I know to do is love him through it.

Thank you all for your continued support, love, and prayers. It's going to be a long six weeks.

It's been six weeks – and an interesting six weeks at that. Let's start with the good news.

Our middle son Austin graduated from high school!! *Best part?* Tony was here to see it. This time last year, I wasn't so sure he would see Austin cross that stage. But, he did. The night Austin graduated Tony said, "Lord, please let me be here to see my little ones graduate." Aydin and Ashton still have eight and ten years respectively until their graduation days come. I listened to his prayer, and quietly thought, "Thank you Lord for keeping him here for today." Often times we forget to say thank you. Thank you to our friends and family. Thank you to our doctors and nurses. And many times, we forget to thank the good Lord upstairs for answering those prayers.

A week before Austin's graduation Tony was pretty sick. We didn't understand why he was getting sicker when he was off chemo except that meant the chemo was working and this break was allowing the cancer to spread. So it was back to Duke we go. They admitted him for some tests to include a spinal tap. Three days before graduation we got the negative results. The fear was that the cancer had spread to his spinal fluid. It had not.

But why was Tony still sick?

The weekend after Austin's graduation was busy. Ashton's birthday, Father's Day, and Austin's grad party. Tony hardly participated. He was in bed most of the weekend. My gut was in knots.

That Monday we went back to Duke. Of course his labs looked great, but Tony, not so much. Tony was adamant about going back on chemo. He said, "I know what happens to people who stop chemo. This is my life we are talking about." I had never heard Tony be so stern about his health. The problem was though, he had maxed out his other chemo FOLFOX (5FU and Oxaliplatin).

I asked what would be next? I was told Irinotecan. "That's an older chemo right?" I asked. And in fact it was. I also said, what about scans? Don't we want a baseline before we start a new drug? We were told to come back the next day for scans and chemo. UGH! Driving and hour and a half home, just to drive all the way back the next day.

The next morning, while Tony was waiting on chemo, they did scans. Tony started the new drug and within minutes started feeling horribly sick. They gave him another drug which abated the side effects and he felt better. All the while in the back of my head I'm thinking, "What are the results of those scans?"

"What about that spot in his lung?"

"What exactly are we dealing with here?"

The results came in just as I emailed the doc. I couldn't believe what I was reading. The spot that had doubled in size from March to May in his right lung was gone.

It was a miracle!

I continued to read the scan. Then I saw it. A new spot doubled in size on his left lung. I immediately called his doc. She explained to me that it could be inflammation but there is really no way of knowing and that we will just have to continue to watch it.

They use the term Wax and Wane.

I continued to read but there was really nothing to discuss. I had concerns about the slowing down of his bowels and some bile duct dilation, both of which can cause obstructions.

We don't need that right now, or ever, to be honest.

Before I knew it, it was time to go home and time to share the next chapter of our journey with the kids. I called them all into the living room and said, "Dad's going back on chemo. Matter of fact, he had it today. "Their faces all dropped and they just looked devastated. I said, "It's back to Duke every two weeks. I want you all to be prepared. He may lose his hair this time." That hit them harder. It's easier to pretend that Daddy's not sick when he doesn't, "look," sick. Alec was on a cruise, so I wasn't able to tell him until today. His response, "Why?" Understandably, he was not happy about the news.

Aydin on the other hand has been doing lots of thinking. The other night he was lying on the couch with tears in his eyes. I asked what was wrong and he told me he's been thinking about what life would be like if daddy, well...you know mom...died. I took a deep breath, fought back the tears, and decided to share in his fear and acknowledge it.

I told him that even though none of us are promised tomorrow, that I too have the same fear. I told him we can be scared together so that we don't have to feel this way or be scared alone. He also asked me what Tony was like before he got sick. What kind of daddy he was. That really started to put more of his feelings and fears into perspective. I asked the older boys to share stories of their childhoods with Tony with Aydin and Ashton. These stories are important and so are the memories.

To sum it all up: I've also learned this is the nature of the beast of stage IV. Some scans will be good. Some won't be. Sometimes spots pop up. And sometimes, they don't. The truth is, I fully acknowledge there will be an end one day, but it doesn't mean I have to live all our life like that's the only reality. We wake up. We put both feet on the floor. And we continue on with our journey. What is the famous saying? Life is a gift, that's why its called the present.

Back To The Hospital

It's been a looooong week.

First I can't thank everyone enough for all the get well cards and notes, gift cards, helping at the house, prayers, and more, this week. Our warrior has been through Hell and back from his liver enzymes being elevated, white blood cell count bottoming out, to poking and prodding.

Test after test, and what do the doctors know? Nothing really. The hard part is noone knows because Tony's cancer hides and only offers symptoms.

Tony went into the hospital Monday after a Duke ER visit suggested by his oncologist. Tony did not look so good. He was in excruciating pain, low BP, and his labs were not pretty. On top of that, he had finished a new round of chemo about a week prior making it hard to know if what was going on was chemo or something else.

Tuesday morning Tony had a barium swallow study that showed he has rediculous esophageal spasms. Well Duh! I knew that doc. That's not the issue.

Tony had a dilated liver bile duct and his LFTs (Liver Function Tests) were a bit elevated but, with the power of God and prayer, they returned to normal in two days.

He also had a scope done with biopsies Thursday morning and we hope to have the results next week. The doctors started him on a new medication last night that should stop all the spasms that are going on from his esophagus down to his large intestine. That may or may not be the culprit, but it can't hurt to try. The drug will counteract any of the effects of the opioids he is on for pain and initiate withdrawal from his gut.

Yes you read right, *initiate withdrawl*.

It was a long night, but Tony is strong and was able to get through it. If the opioids that they have him on have caused this, Tony should experience some relief in the next few days. If not, well then I fear the worst – his cancer has spread.

At the end of the day, the good news is while he was in the hospital his blood pressure is now back to normal. He's hydrated. He and I have some one-on-one time and, believe it or not, much needed rest.

We hope to come home from the hospital today. Tony is ready and, honestly, so am I. I know the kids are ready. It's been a long week. I miss them dearly. If you're gonna be sick, and the docs can't fix it, we'd rather be sick at home.

So where are we? Well, we are just going to keep taking one day at a time and keep treating the symptoms. That's all we really can do. I trust our team of doctors. I just do not trust the data from the tests. That is a hard place to be in. I will write more later, but for now, this is where we are.

The Chemo Is Killing Him

I don't know what it's like to lose a husband. I don't know what it's like to lose a child. Right now I just know the pain of losing a brother. Everything else has been in the natural order of things.

What I do know is fear.

Fear what it's going to be like without Tony. Guilt for thinking about it. Grief of a past life. And, anger for cancer making me feel all of this. I feel like I've been given a curfew that isn't fair. A curfew that I know exists, but no one will tell me the time.

A month ago we tried a new chemo. Tony was adamant about trying chemo again. He said a break in chemo would kill him. He said he knows what has happened to others when they stop chemo. I disagreed. I felt as if the chemo was making him sicker, weaker, and causing him to lose weight. However, Tony was pretty determined to give it one more shot, and so we did.

Monday he weighed in at 138 pounds at Duke. A seven pound weight loss in two weeks. His oncologist turned his chemo down in hopes that he could maintain his weight and be able to tolerate this new drug.

By Thursday Tony was in uncontrollable pain. When it's that bad, certain meds help him sleep through the pain. Saturday morning I convinced Tony to get on the scale. My fear was spot on, Tony had lost 12 pounds in just six days. At the same time his oncologist had emailed me asking for an update. We discussed the past few days and then I saw the last sentence in her email. *"Regarding Chemo - No More."*

Tony is not able to tolerate anymore chemo. Honestly, we are reluctant to try anything else. Now I'm in totally uncharted territory.

We have been fighting this fight for over six years. We are literally treating an invisible cancer. I truly hate not having a plan. I hate not being able to physically see what we are treating. It's hard to know what is the right decision to make. I fear that the chemo is going to take him before the cancer will. But, if he doesn't have chemo, it's only a matter of time.

So what do we do?

Well, Monday we go back to Duke for labs, fluids, chest x-ray, and a quick visit with the doc, and go from there.

I know he's physically tired, but mentally he's very much still there and wanting to fight. He's loving, kind, gentle, and still spending time with the boys. He's making those times special. He tells me not to worry, that's he's OK. He allows the boys to play on his phone while laying in his armpit.

The boys just want – need – that time with him. It doesn't have to be anything extravagant. Just allowing that time to happen. It means going to bed late, and sharing your bed with the kiddos. It means dinner in bed with daddy, crumbs in the sheets, and a young one on my side of the bed. These memories will be what matters. So with that said, I'm ending this with, instead of typing, I'm going to join Tony and the boys in bed, and treasure every moment, beause at the end of the day, that's all any of us have.

PRAY FOR OUR HERO, OUR WARRIOR, OUR LOVE!! #TEAMTONY

When Daddy Meets Jesus

My 10-year-old, Aydin, and I had quite the conversation last week. It went like this:

Me: "*Aydin, Do you have any questions about what is going on with Daddy?*"

Aydin: "*Ummm...yeah, actually. When does daddy have chemo again?*"

It hit me, that Aydin was not aware that we were not going to do any more chemo.

Me: "*Well baby, daddy isn't going to get any chemo for a while.*"

Aydin sat there looking around the room. You could tell he was thinking.

Me: "*Do you have another question?*"

Aydin: "*Yes...so...if daddy isn't going to be getting chemo, what is going to keep him alive?*"

Me (Deep Breath): "*Well baby, we just need to pray. Pray that daddy can get stronger and maybe gain some weight.*"

Aydin still had a look of thought on his face.

Me: "*What are you thinking about buddy?*"

Aydin: "*What it's going to be like...ya know.*"

Me:" *I know sweetie. I think about that too sometimes.*"

Aydin: "*Mommy? Daddy's side of the bed is going to be empty.*"

All I could do was wrap my son in his arms and say, "*You can lay there if you want to. One day, daddy is going to get to meet Jesus.*

He is going to prepare heaven for us and be ready to take us home when it's our turn. And the truth is, none of us know when that will be. Isn't daddy lucky that he knows that heaven isn't so far away so that he can do all the things he's ever wanted to do before then? It's kinda neat right?"

We all say, what would you do if you knew the apocalypse was coming? So, why can't you ask the same question when you are told you have cancer? Because with cancer comes a fight. But, sometimes, that fight is painful. Sometimes that fight makes you tired and you lose who you are. And its OK to say, "Jesus, Take me Home." One day, my dear hubby will meet our creator. He will be reunited with his brother, him mom, and his dad. I don't know when that day will be. I just pray that I have the strength to keep my family together and Band-Aid their hearts, even if it's just for a moment. I want my boys to feel at peace because their daddy is no longer in pain. I don't want people to forget about my boys. I want them to still have a cheering section in the stands. I want people to treat them like the *normal* kids they are. And, most importantly, I want my boys to live and to succeed on their own terms.

So, where are we in the journey?

Tony has developed aspiration pneumonia again. His liver enzymes have doubled in two weeks. Tony's white blood cell count is 17.6 (normal is 4.0). Physically, he has been very tired and sleeping a lot. Mentally, his fight is still on and strong. Friday is a big day for us. We have scans and come up with a plan. A plan that doesn't include chemo.

Saturday the boys come home from Camp Kesem. For those that don't know what that is, it's a camp for kids whose parents have been effected by cancer. It is put on by college students across the country and is free to the campers. [Visit: http://campkesem.org]

But really it's a place for the kids to get a break from what's going on at home and just be kids for a while. I just want my younger boys to laugh, and smile, and not have a worry on their mind, even if it's just for a moment.

The Results Are In - After 19 Days!!!

Follow your gut.

That's all I can say.

I knew something was wrong. I could feel it. I just knew it. But, nobody believed me. We spent a week in the hospital two months ago and they couldn't find anything. Yet my gut was once again in knots. Two months of the same thing. Tony is in intense pain, throwing up everything he put down. Nothing made sense. It was time for routine scans and the CT showed an obstruction in his small bowel. The worst part? It was on the outside pushing in and no one could see what it was.

Tony's oncologist called his surgeon and they discussed a plan. Tony was to have an upper and lower GI scope to determine next steps. But, most likely, Tony was going to need another surgery.

Between being told no more chemo and Tony being so sick, we decided it was time for Tony to see everyone. All of our friends and family came over for a great Sunday dinner taking photos and lifting Tony's spirits. Little did they know about his recent obstruction and possible surgery. And, neither did the kids. Tony didn't just have an obstruction, he was also recovering from aspiration pneumonia.

I have never been so scared, or so I thought.

Monday I got Tony's scopes scheduled. He was to start his prep Wednesday. But, low and behold, Tony walked into the kitchen Tuesday night and said, I think we need to go to the hospital.

Tony never says that! He hates the hospital!

I paged his oncologist and she called back right back. She said to get Tony to the Duke ER A.S.A.P. She was afraid his obstruction had worsened.

We got to Duke and went straight back to a room. XRAY's, labs etc. Tony's liver enzymes had skyrocketed. I mean 12 to 212, and pancreatic enzymes, 16 to 637.

My heart was racing.

The attending physician came in and I demanded a CT, explained what we had learned just four days earlier. Tony had a CT and it showed the obstruction had, in fact, worsened. Doc came in and said, I paged the surgeon on call to see if you're going straight to an OR or a room upstairs.

Um…yeah…so…you are only paging his surgeon, not just some resident on call. When I told him who Tony's surgeon was, the team came down right away. Because Tony was stable, and his surgeon would be arriving in 90 min, we felt it could wait.

I called my mom in tears. "Mom, I don't know what's going on. I'm so scared. Everything is a mess. His pancreas and liver are acting up. He's in so much pain mom." Worse, we still didn't know what was causing the obstruction. I just knew it was causing major issues.

Good news, no surgery that night. going upstairs and waiting for consult with "The Man."

Surgery was scheduled for the following Friday, , but Tony wasn't healthy enough. He was so malnourished on a scale from 18-

45, Tony was a 7. That's when we learned that Tony was to start TPN and had to stay in the hospital until surgery. Then, we needed another seven to ten days for him to recover and get healthy. I had *no* idea how to tell the little ones. I had *no* idea how I was going to do it.

I had *no* idea about anything at this point.

After talking to Tony, we decided I needed to go home for a couple of days and break the news in person. On the way home, my best friend called me. She was coming to help for as long as we needed her too. She was my angel.

I pulled into the driveway, and surprised the boys. "Wait. Where's daddy, mommy? Ashton asked. My heart sunk. I told them to get out of the pool and dry off and come inside.

Daddy's going to be in the hospital for a little while. "How long mommy?" he asked. "A couple more weeks baby," I answered.

Aydin ran upstairs and Ashton started to cry. Austin fought his tears, and I could see he wasn't happy. I mean who would be right?

That night, I crawled into bed...and his side of the bed was empty.

A week of me going back and forth to the hospital went by. Now it was time for surgery. The surgery was a success, but when I asked about the obstruction, the surgeon didn't have an answer for me. He told me pathology would tell us for sure. At this point we were to focus on nutrition and recovery.

But me, I only cared about pathology. Was it cancer? or not?

Tony was doing great for the first couple of days and then he took a quick turn and not for the good. He began to sleep, and sleep, and sleep. He couldn't hold a conversation and, when he was awake, he was staring into space. When it was time to eat, he just had absolutely no desire for food. A couple of bites, and he wanted me to take the tray away. His color was no longer good, and I felt like I was losing him. For days I said, something is wrong. For days I said, we are missing something. For days, I relived what I went through with my mother-in-law, watching her die.

Palliative care was called. I told the doctor what was going on. He asked me what I needed to know. "I need to know if my husband is dying and no one is telling me," I blurted out, tears pouring down my face.

I just need to know!

The palliative care doctor put his hand on my hand and said, "I don't think that is what is going on here. I really don't." I looked up and said, "Really?" He said, "No. I think this is from medication, something we did, and we can fix it." We went through every little medication, change, add, removal, etc. over the past few days. I said, "Wait, they increased his pump on Monday." So we decided to decrease his pain pump, and turn off the rest of the meds.

The next day, Tony came a little more alert, but still had no appetite. I had palliative care paged and said, "I don't understand." The same doctor and I had another great conversation about quality of life and family and how Tony just wants to go home. "We miss our kids, our family, our home," we told him.

Just then we had some great visitors, and we all went down to get lunch. While we were sitting there, I received an email from Tony's surgeon.

Good news Intraoperative biopsies did not show cancer, just scar tissue. Ted Pappas

I gasped for air.

I couldn't believe it.

I turned my phone and showed it to Tony. Then Frank, then April. Suddenly, we were all smiling. I forwarded the message on to his oncologist. When I turned around, who did I see in the cafeteria, but his oncologist. I said, "Did you hear? Did you get my message?" She hadn't, I shared the news and we shared a big hug and celebrated right where we were standing.

It was the best news, ever!

I replied to his surgeon and said, "OMG! OMG! OMG! Really?" followed by, "Does that mean we can go home now?"

"Yes. Tomorrow," he replied. "With or without TPN?" I asked. "Without," he answered. "Yes!" I typed. "Happy Day! Happy Day! ThankYou! Thank You! Thank You!"

SO WITHOUT FURTHER ADIEU, I AM HAPPY TO SHARE THAT AFTER 19 DAYS AT DUKE UNIVERSITY HOSPITAL, TONY LEONARD AND I WILL BE GOING HOME!!!

We are surprising our boys at their first football game tomorrow, so please don't spoil the surprise!!!

We can't thank you all enough for the *incredible* support. The visitors. The gift cards. Donations. Meals. It's all just been amazing. Tony's journey and recovery is far from over. He is still very malnourished, and weak. But, we can continue recovering while improving nutrition at home. I can't wait to sleep in the same bed with my love again.

With that said, to my fellow caregivers. Don't *ever* stop advocating for your loved ones. When you feel something is wrong, stomp those feet. Follow your gut. Family time is important. Don't be afraid to accept and ask for help. Demand the best. And most importantly, believe in God and miracles.

They really do happen every day!

Losing Faith...

Once upon a time, there was a little girl who always needed to have the closet light on when she went to sleep. She was afraid of her closet when it was dark. The door needed to be cracked just a bit so the light would act as a night light. See…the monsters don't come out in the light. They only come out in the dark. They come out when no one is looking, when no one is watching, when your guard is down.

As the little girl got older she knew she could take on any monsters in her closet and learned to trust her gut, her strength, and face those monsters head on if they should ever appear. The now not-so-young woman learned to sleep in the dark soundly, peacefully, and without fear.

Just then, when she least expect it, the monsters would bang on the closet door and try to come out and scare her, but the now woman would simply take a deep breath, and turn on the light. For the light of the angles always protected her.

See there were no monsters, just fear. But our fears always come out when we keep the light of God off. Her strength was so powerful, she forgot that God had given it to her.

And that my friends is where I am today. I am struggling today. I am struggling with trusting that light. Every night before bed, I turn off the lights. I don't pray any more. I ask others to pray for me, because I'm afraid if I do pray, my prayers will be questions. My ask will scare me, and His answer? Yeah, well, I'm afraid of that too.

I *refuse* to ask God, "Why?" Because, every day my love wakes up, sips on his coffee, and makes plans to go out *Every day* – no matter how tired he is. Even if it's a trip down the street to Dollar General with the boys. Tony finds a way to make each and every day count. So who am I? Who am I to deny my love that memory or moment with his children?

Prime example: last Saturday Tony decided to take the boys hunting. Now I can't get those two knuckleheads up on a school morning at 6:00 a.m. but, come Saturday morning at 4:30 a.m. they were up and dressed and waking us up to go hunting.

Now I was *mad*. I knew darn well it was too cold and Tony didn't need to climb up a deer stand. I was so afraid he was going to fall. Then a friend reminded me, "Christy, even if its for five minutes, don't take that memory away from him or the boys." And, he was right.

See lately, I've been living in fear, waiting for the other shoe to drop. I've been living like that for a long time. The light has been off, the night is pitch black, and the monsters are gathering strength in the closet. See sometimes I get mad at God. But, that only means that I know he's there right? I mean, I'm sure I've made him mad a few times. I don't understand his plan or his reasons, and then I get a text message about how Tony offers hope. Or, today during his CT scan, a man said, "See, he's a walking miracle and a testament to what our God can do." And that my friends is why I'm afraid to pray. Because I want him healed, and I'm afraid that in order to heal him, I'll have to let him go, and I'm not ready. My boys aren't ready. *We* #TEAMTONY are *not* ready.

You see, Tony's birthday is coming up. Our 5th annual Stomach Cancer golf tournament and charity dinner is coming up. Our warrior is *celebrating life* with another birthday!!

Come join us. Come join him. Every birthday for him is a miracle.

Tony had his CT scan today. Now we have more tests. We have MRIs next week. Tony's had some funky things going on with him lately and well, his body may say one thing, but his *mind* says something completely different. And, as his wife, I will continue to stand by and fight and advocate and care for him as long as he allows me to. Our warrior is getting thin. Our warrior may be tired. But our warrior is going to fight until it's time for him to join that protecting light.

Waiting Is The Hardest Part

Monday, October 29, 2018

I'm sitting here waiting.

Waiting because the next 24 hours will tell me what our fate is.

Tony was admitted back into the hospital yesterday. I don't want to go into detail because part of this journey is keeping as much dignity for your loved one intact as possible.

With that said, I went downstairs to get our coffee this morning, and on the way back they were taking him down for his MRI. The two-hour long MRI that would tell us if Tony's cancer has spread to his spine. The symptoms are there, but we just don't know. Tony has diffused cancer, and it doesn't like to show up on scans.

But something isn't right and we all know it.

Tony's malnutrition labs are right back to where they were a couple of months ago. My heart is breaking for him. Hell, my heart is breaking for me. I don't want to be selfish but it hurts. I haven't been able to stop crying since I got into it with God yesterday. I yelled at him. I told him. "I didn't ask for this - any of this! I didn't ask for this life, and I don't want it! What did I do to you?" Then I called him an SOB. I know, I'm not supposed to go there, but damnit my gut has been in knots and my chest hurts, and until they tell me different, I know there is something wrong.

So back to the room I went...alone...watching the second hand tick on the clock. Looking at my phone to see if there was a text message or two not about Tony that could help me keep my mind off things. Wanting to cry with someone, but instead, I do what I always do. Focus on other things like our golf tournament this weekend, the boys school, work, anything. But, honestly, I can't help but stare at the door and hope someone walks through with the verdict. As I type this, the man in the white coat is standing outside the door.

Careful what you wish for.

My heart is racing, beating super fast. Come out with it already. The doc and PA are standing there and tell me his brain looked fine. We got the all clear. But his spine results weren't back yet.

What could be causing all these issues Tony is having? What is the answer going to be, good, bad, indifferent? Not wanting the cancer, but wanting an answer so we can treat/fix it.

If the cancer is in his spine, then the journey is coming to an end. If it's not, then what do we do so he won't starve to death? Someone please guide me. I don't know what the right answer is.

I made a mistake yelling at God. But I know he knows I didn't really mean it. I'm just wanting answers. Answers that will fix Tony, fix me, fix our family. I ask him what's wrong, and he just shakes his head. He's so tired. I am too. I am straight-up exhausted. But I can't give up. Not today. Not tomorrow. Not ever!

When Is It All Too Much?

I'm sitting here in this hospital room again, writing one of the hardest blog posts I've ever put on paper. For some reason, when we think something, it doesn't seem real unless you say it. But, even then, it still can be altered.

However, when you put something on paper, it's like it was etched in stone.

I have been very quiet these past couple of months.

I have talked about long hospital stays, the waiting game, the ups-and-downs. What I haven't talked about is *my* journey. Where am I at.

I am struggling.

I am struggling with what the right answer is.

So many times these past couple of days I have just wanted to disconnect Tony from these IV's and take him home, put him in our bed, and just allow him to live or die...whatever God has planned.

Then I look at my boys with him. I look at how they smile with him. How it doesn't matter *what* they are doing as long as they can curl up next to their daddy and just spend time with him. Because honestly, that's all any of us want. More time. More time, but at what cost? I have sat back and watched Tony go through test after test after test and had things poked and examined, that *no* person should have to go through.

For what? Five more weeks? Five more months? Five more days? Or, maybe just five more hours. Five more minutes. Five more seconds.

Are we just spinning our wheels doc? Because I am struggling here. I am going against *everything* I promised him and myself we would do. I never said I would just keep putting him through this if it wasn't going to change the outcome.

I am hurting inside because I have no idea which direction to take. I don't want to lose him, I don't want to let my boys down. I don't want anyone to think I gave up or failed him. I don't want to rob this precious time they have with each other. And honestly, selfishly, I don't want to be alone. I don't want his side of the bed to be empty forever. I want to keep fussing at him for leaving his clothes on the bathroom floor and I truly, honestly – here's something most of you don't know – but I really don't want to love someone more than myself again only to have to let them go ever again.

My chest hurts. My eyes burn. My head is pounding. I feel like I'm drowning. There is no right or wrong answer. No one is going to come out of this on top.

Why?

Why am I feeling this way?

I haven't shared a reason. Tony's MRI scans were clean. I couldn't believe it. I had mentally prepared myself for hospice. I was ready.

I knew what I was going to say to the boys and our family and friends. I was prepared. When we got the news that everything was fine, I said, "That's great," but then added, "Then why the Hell is all of this happening?" in a voice so deep in my head, nobody else could hear it.

For the past eight weeks Tony has had some personal issues killing his dignity. These past two weeks his bowels stopped moving. In hopes that everything that he was experiencing was a result of malnutrition, we agreed that Total Parenteral Nutrician (TPN) was the way to go. TPN is an IV method of feeding that bypasses his digestive tract all together. Tony was supposed to be admitted Sunday to start TPN in the hospital. Then we would go home after a week. Instead, he woke up Thursday morning with his belly distended. Not too, too much, but enough for me to notice and call the doctors. They moved his admission up to that same day.

His CT, of course, showed not evidence of disease, just a slight increase in ascites. We agreed this was due to malnutrition and started TPN immediately. In the meantime they tried shots and suppositories to help his bowels move, but nothing happened. They had him pee in a cup, examined his male parts, prostate exam, and more. They consulted with urology and wanted to scope his bladder. When I learned what that entailed, I said, "*Stop!* Hasn't this man been through enough?" His surgeon, who has been with us for these past seven years, came in and I broke down and cried.

When is enough, enough?

Tony has been poked and prodded in places *no* man should *ever* be. What is our goal here doc? And what are you not telling me? His response was, "Let's see what the tests show. I'll talk with your oncologist this afternoon." He agreed Tony is my husband, a daddy, and not a guinea pig.

The lesson here is don't be afraid to draw a line in the sand. Don't be afraid to ask for a goal. *Make sure* you aren't spending what might be your last days grasping for straws and putting your love through unnecessary tests. Lay in the bed with one another. Kiss often. Follow your gut and speak up. Quality over Quantity.

...When Your Gut Is Right

Why did I say Christmas?

Why was that always what stuck out in my mind?

I told them...I told them they can't find it. *The cancer is there. You just can't see it!* I mean I get it – diffused cancer it doesn't show on scans. But he can't poop doc! He throws it all up doc! He is in pain doc!

Something is wrong! Very, very wrong!

"It's an obstruction," the doc says. "No cancer Ms. Leonard."

"Then fix it!" I demand...And so it was.

"Doc, he can't control his bladder. He's only 45 doc. What's wrong doc? It's the cancer. I'm telling you."

"Ms. Leonard, we don't see any cancer."

"Then what's wrong?"

"He tested positive for a UTI. Antibiotics are waiting for him at the pharmacy."

"DOC...He can't control his bowels. IT'S THE CANCER...I know it is."

"Christy, I'm admitting him and we will scan his spine...prepare yourself."

Back to Duke for a three hour MRI.

Me: "I'm ready Doc, just tell me."

"SCANS ARE CLEAR! WHAT??? SERIOUSLY??? THEN WHAT'S WRONG?? IT'S THE CANCER I KNOW IT IS."

Doc: "Ms. Leonard we think its his nutrition. Let's start TPN."

"Happy Birthday Tony! Time to start TPN." I thought to myself.

"When do you want to come to the hospital? The doctor asked.

"Can it be after the boys football game this weekend?" he answers. "It's the second round of the playoffs and I don't want him to miss it."

"Absolutely," the doc says.

"Doc!! He's projectile vommitting. His belly is swollen! What do I do Doc?" I ask.

"I'm admitting him Christy," he says.

"No!" I protest, "He's going to miss the game!"

"Christy, get it together," he said. And so I did.

"All this poking and prodding Doc...tell me...*Tell Me!*"

"We don't have results yet," he said.

"Then I'm going home for a couple of days to be with my boys," I say. "I love you honey. See you Thursday Doc."

The phone rings when I get home. It's a conversation I've dreaded.

Me: "Yes Doc?"

Doc: "Are you home?"

Me: "Yes."

Doc: "Are you with the boys?"

Me: "Yes, but they are in the other room."

Doc: "I'm sorry to do this over the phone..."

Me: "No Doc, say it ain't so..."

Doc: "His ascites tested positive for cancer cells..."

Me: "NO...NO...NO!!!!!!!!!!"

Doc: "I am so sorry Christy."

Me: "WHY DOC...HE FOUGHT SO HARD!!"

But...I knew. I knew all this time. My gut told me so.

"You were right...you were right all along," he said.

"I don't want you to tell him, not without me Doc," I ordered. "*Not one person!* I'll be there in the morning."

As I hung up someone reached into my gut, punched me so hard I thought I would pass out from the pain, grabbed my heart and ripped it out.

"*Why God?*" I screamed. "*Why? Way are you taking my love from me? Why are you taking my babbies' Daddy? What did he ever do to you?! He's a good man, God. Why are you doing this to me? First you took my brother. Then you took my father-in-law. Then my mother-in-law. Why are you taking him from our family?*

It hurts!

I'm drowning.

I can't breath.

The tears are pouring for the hundred thousandth time and I have never felt so helpless in my life. Then I take a deep breath and email the doc, "What are our options Doc?"

"Tony's too weak for treatment, the recommendation is Hospice," he replied.

NOOOOOOOOOOOOOOOOOOOOOOOOO!!!!!!!

Any tiny piece of my heart that was left fell to the floor and with each tear my heart shattered.

All I can think about now is, "Dear God, how do I tell my boys?"

Please pray for all of us.

I still haven't told my little ones. I don't know how. I am numb. Now my love is aware that his journey is coming to an end. A journey that he and I both fought so hard to continue untill we were 100 years old. My love. My best friend. My everything. A piece of me will die with you...I will never be the same.

But I promise you this, everyone in this world will know about stomach cancer.

And I promise you this, with every breath I take, our boys will remember their Daddy. We will continue to fight for all those that fight this disease.

Your legacy will be amazing! And you will forever be close to me. I promise you this with all my heart.

XOXOX

Everyday Is A Gift

We told the boys. It was gut wrenching. It was harder than hard. Aydin, now 10, yells, *"No! No! No! Mommy! No!"* And runs down the hallway. Meanwhile Ashton, now eight, throws himself on his Daddy's chest crying, *"What does that mean? What does that mean?"*

The four of us cried. And then I took a deep breath and said, "It means no more hospital stays. No more doctors. No more poking. No more surgeries. It means we can be home as a family!"

The boys stopped crying and said, "Yes!!!" Kids are amazing!! They remind us that we *have* to look at the bright side of things.

Within every fog there are always blessings.

We received letters from Duke to give to the boys' school so it would be patient for any missed days or assignments. I was however, still going to try and keep things as normal as possible.

After about a week of coming home early from school and having a messy house, it was, "Come to Jesus," time. I lined them up and said, "Boys, I get it. We got some really crappy news. But you know what? The sun comes up and the moon will too. And the dishwasher still has to be unloaded and loaded. The trash, still needs to make it to the curb. Our lives *still* go on. We don't just *stop* living and doing what needs to be done. We are *not* going to just sit around and wait for daddy's end."

The next week Tony went from rocky to stable. He didn't need his oxygen as much. He was getting around more, wanting to go out shopping. He even bought a new handgun. I mean really, what am I supposed to say, No?

Our family stopped grieving, and started *living* again. Tony even made it to Aydin's state Championship game. Not only did he make it...*We Won!* Aydin played one of his best games ever.

This will be a short entry today because I'm spending more time with Tony and my boys. Tony's hospice agency granted Tony's final wish, to see Aydin play in Florida at Nationals.

Tony is living! He will not lay down!

Just because Hospice is here does *not* mean you die tomorrow. It means you *enjoy life comfortably*. I wish sometimes we had brought hospice in earlier because Tony is finally not in as much pain as he was. He can receive medications without fail or questions. I have help if need be. We have nurses who are members of our family now. Oxygen delivered same day. Shower chairs. Wound care. Our warrior is *not* giving up y'all, he is *still living*.

Yes, he is tired. Yes, he is weak. But his mind is full and present and loving. Yes, Tony is losing weight and has issues with eating. But that's not what this is about. This is about making each day a *gift*. A *treasure*. A *blessing*.

My Tony is strong in his heart and mind. I'd rather have that, than anything else!

We can't ever thank everyone enough for the love and support that we have received over the past month.

Tony said, "I've never felt so loved in all my life." Help in the form of donations from MealTrain©, household supplies from the stomach cancer warriors group, and Debbie's Dream Foundation's continuous support and understanding. Help from my parents and my best friend Nikki who dropped everything to let me cry and be selfish.

And, for all the newly diagnosed, I'm sorry you are going through this. Welcome to the club. *You are not alone.* Tony has had seven *amazing* years and is still holding on. Don't give up hope. Treasure each moment. Live each day as fully as you can. And, when you are tired, remember it's OK to be tired. You are not weak. In fact, you are all the stronger for admitting you're tired. *I love you all!*

Our journey isn't over!

Hospice, Heartache, and Healing

Saturday, December 29, 2018

We are exactly at one month of hospice. It's actually a lot better than we thought. At first we didn't think he was going to make it through the weekend. All of our friends came over. It was great. We had food and fun. The kids were wondering what everyone was doing here. I didn't have the heart to tell them what was going on at the time.

Tony needed oxygen and hospice had moved in so quickly. I think what had gotten to me more than anything else was when they said it was going to be fast. I guess they didn't know my Tony. He never let anything go quickly. He sure as heck wasn't going to give up.

There were still things that needed to be said. Places to go. People that we needed to see. That's when I decided we were going to *enjoy* hospice. We were *not* going to just sit here and watch Tony fade. We were going to *live*. Tony got to make it to Aydin's football games. He got to teach Austin how to fix up his truck. He got to snuggle up with Ashton He enjoyed time with his granddaughters, time with Anthoney and Alec; everyone.

Tony even had the opportunity to sit down with the boys and express his expectations after he's gone. Remind them we are still a family even though he's gone. *Nothing* will ever change that!! I think what was almost more important, was the fact that we got to spend time as whole family unit – as the *Leonards*.

Christmas Eve: They were all here. No pictures. No poses. Just hot dogs. Marshmallows. Pajamas. Laughs. And even some tears. You can't expect a night with five brothers to go completely smoothly can you?

My parents came and mom forgot the presents an hour away. My dad graciously went and retrieved them. The look on the older boys faces were priceless. *Who does that?*

A great husband, father, and grandfather does.

It's teaching life by example. Tony and I got to enjoy it all together. Aydin got a little upset when we pulled out old family videos and pictures because he told me it wasn't fair that he wouldn't be able to do that. I said, "Aydin, you have *your own* memories and daddy will still be at everything and in everything *you* do and *we do.*"

I truly wanted them to all make memories. I wanted to give them the chance to say "I'm sorry." "I love you." And anything that they felt they needed to say. Instead my little ones, (I sometimes wish they didn't know) have fears that they didn't have before.

Ashton often says, Daddy, "I don't want to lose you," and breaks down. He gets mad when people come to visit because he feels they are taking time away from his time. But at the end of the day, I remind him that none of us are promised tomorrow, so if you want to snuggle up with me or daddy, *do it.*

Aydin, I have found, has become my protector. He doesn't like to see me upset. He makes comments like, "Good to see you eating mom," or "Ashton, don't be disrespectful." One night Aydin got mad at Tony and ran into my office yelling, "I hate him Mom!"

"No you don't," I said. "You hate what the cancer has done to him." He looked at me, and a tear fell from his eye. I said, "Aydin, if I told you that dad just took his last breath, you would never be able to live with yourself for what you just said." He agreed, and I told him, "Now dry those eyes, apologize, and tell him you love him." See, that's a normal life lesson. Suck it up. Apologize. Move on.

Raising the boys and teaching them right from wrong doesn't stop just because Tony is sick, it just hits them with a deeper reality. Christmas morning was no different than last year, except I only made frozen pizzas for dinner.

I'm sorry I needed a break. The next day Anthoney and Akiya brought our granddaughters over. We made slime, it was so much fun. All the boxes were checked. The list was about complete. And Tony has begun to decline.

Please pray for all of us. We are on hard times.

I'm Not Ready To Say Goodbye

Wednesday, January 02, 2019

Many people have asked me, "Have you told him it's OK to go?"

No! No !

I haven't.

I can't.

I think about what I'll say, or how I will say it, and then I break down. I don't want to accept that he will be gone forever. I don't want to be strong anymore, and this will take all the strength I have. What will I have left for the boys?

I turned on our wedding song. I said, "Dance with me." He took me in his boney arms, and for a minute the world stood still. We kissed. We hugged. We swayed. We cried.

How do I tell the man that finds the strength to dance with me that he can go dance in heaven?

I have planned the funeral/celebration of life. I know what pictures I want to use. I have discussed it with his best friends. But, I can't tell him good bye. I know he's tired, and I know he's holding on for me.

Once upon a time, I thought our love could beat anything, that it could survive anything, and that maybe, just maybe, our love could even beat cancer. How can you love someone enough to tell them good bye...forever?

We were supposed to grow old together.

We were supposed to renew our vows.

179

We were supposed to argue about money more.

We were supposed to laugh more.

We were robbed.

I didn't choose this. We didn't leave each other. There wasn't a big fight. So, how do I send him on his way?

I can't tell him I'll be okay, because I won't be. I can promise him that I will raise our boys how he wanted them to be raised. I can promise him that he will be a part of *everything* we do. I can promise him that I will miss him and that I will love him forever. I can promise him that his legacy will continue to inspire so many. I can promise him that Tony Leonard will become a household name. Because trust me, the world *will* know about stomach cancer *and* Tony Leonard!!!

Tony's journey is coming to a rapid end. He has developed a Kennedy Terminal Ulcer (KTU), a dark sore that develops rapidly during the final stages of a person's life. Kennedy ulcers grow as skin breaks down as part of the dying process.

I discovered it last night. His nurse told me what it was this morning. It completely broke my heart. I now know we are looking at days. His blood pressure and oxygen continue to be low. But my love continues to force himself out of bed. My love is so strong. He is *not weak. Not ever, not now.*

Maybe that's what I tell him. No my love, you are not giving up. You are not weak. You are not letting me down. I love you too much to allow you to suffer like this any more. I'm sorry I couldn't save you, I'm sorry we didn't have more time. But *"THANK YOU FOR SPENDING THE REST OF YOUR LIFE WITH ME!"*

It's almost time for you to be reunited with your mom, dad, and brother, my love!! Tell my brothers I love them. Give your parents a hug for me. Please tell your mom I hope I made her proud with my Korean cooking. Tell your dad *I miss him so much*. I never got to say good bye. And, when you get to heaven, my love, save a place for me right next to you, because I will be there with you one day!

For now, I will dry my eyes. Lay in his arms. Kiss him. Tell him I love him and enjoy the time we have, together.

Watching Him Fade...
Piece by Peace

Two short hours after I shared I wasn't ready to say good bye, I received a phone call from Brooke, one of our amazing hospice nurses. She wanted to help Tony and I renew our vows. I couldn't believe it. She said, Friday at 10:00. Pastor Dennis would be officiating. I texted my mom and a few close friends. I pulled out seven suits for Tony, all of them too big. His two best friends came and helped him get dressed. My mom pinned on his boutonniere, all while I was upstairs getting dressed. Years before I had bought a white dress from Ross for about $20 that hung in my closet for the perfect moment.

Friday was that moment.

Brooke's mom did my hair. And, just like eleven and a half years before, my baby sister was right there. She wiped my tears and led the way down the stairs. I can tell you, I didn't notice another person in the room except Tony with our two youngest by his side. It was the older three who stood next to Tony at our first wedding. Having Aydin and Ashton next to him this time, completed everything.

When I saw Tony, my heart broke. Instead of being filled with happiness, I felt dejected.

We were supposed to spend the rest of our lives together.

Grow old together.

Then, when Pastor Dennis started speaking, I looked into Tony's eyes. "I love you," he whispered and I the same. Nothing else mattered at that point, just us loving one another and reminding each other of that.

When we kissed, I felt like it would be the last time – and you know what, it was okay. We were complete. All the hard conversations were over. We renewed our vows. We even smashed cake in each other's faces. My love could've met our Lord and Savior right then and it would've been okay. I will have the *privilege* and *honor* to have been married to my Tony for the rest of his life.

We thought he had days, but those days have again turned into a week, and now weeks. After we renewed our vows. My love started fading even more.

Just when I thought he couldn't lose more weight he did. Just when I thought he couldn't sleep more, he has. And just when I thought I was ready for him to stop suffering...I wasn't.

There is a selfish side to all of this that I don't like to admit. I don't want him to go.

Last night after I helped Tony back from the bathroom, he fell into the bed. He didn't have the strength to move really. So I curled up with him as is. He had the strength to scratch my back. He had the strength to say, "I love you." And, at that moment in time, I was no longer okay with him leaving.

The world stood still at that moment in time.

And, for that moment, there was no cancer. I felt no bones. And we were back to living our happy lives.

Reality struck five minutes later. He had to sit up quickly. He felt sick. The vomiting started. His eyes turned black with lack of oxygen. His weakness was apparent. I was so helpless. "My O2 baby," he gasped. At that moment I remembered how it wasn't fair for him. It's not fair for him to keep holding on for me, for the kids.

He's suffering.

This morning as I was laying in his arms, him holding my hand across his belly he felt my tears on his shoulder. "Don't cry baby," he whispered. "Its going to be OK."

He's never said that before. He always said, "I'll be OK," never, "It."

"I can't do it without you," I said.

"Yes you can, baby," Tony told me. "You're a strong woman." My heart was physically breaking and hurting. I don't want to live without him.

But it's just not fair to him.

Tony's ulcer has gotten worse. It's opening now and his skin is just dying. Tony's not scared. We've checked all the boxes. Every day is a gift. Though he's breaking down piece by piece, *Tony*, my love, my Tony, is finally at *peace* with life, with writing the final chapter. He continues to be strong for all of us. Our journey isn't over, but every morning that he is able to say "I love you," is truly a blessing.

ABC11 Covered Renewal of Vows

You Took Your Last Breath...
It Hurts So Bad

Is it a dream? Maybe you're just away on a business trip. Maybe my phone will ring and your voice is on the other end. I've been pretty numb. For five days I watched your words get fewer, and voice get softer. You moved into a hospital bed right next to our bed of twelve years and I still found a way to cuddle with you every night. You held my hand and held on tight. You were so weak but determined to still get up each day. The last time you stood up you gave me the longest hug we had had in a while.

No words were shared. Just holding one another and not wanting to let go. You were just skin and bones but our hearts were beating together. Your best friends were there every night. You weren't alone. And, every time your breaths would pause, we would hold your hand and tell you it was OK.

But you still weren't ready my love.

What were you holding on for? Aydin, he needed his time. I heard him cry as he said goodbye.

Ashton needed to know that time was getting close. I carefully put him in your armpit as you whispered to him it would be OK. Ashton cried and asked. "Why?"

I had no answers other than, "I don't know baby, but if daddy says we will be okay, we will be okay."

That night, Broin, Frank, and I stayed up with Tony all night. He was restless, waking up and moaning every fifteen minutes.

Alternating the Morphine and Ativan I struggled. Was I killing the love of my life? I had to dig deep because my love told me, "Don't let me lay there and not be able to say I love you. Don't let me lay there and not be able to tell you I was in pain."

My room smelled of death.

Tony's organs were shutting down. His skin was dying. And my love didn't want to be like that. With all his strength he reached out out to our hospice nurse Brooke looking at her like he was begging for relief. Tony was choking on the morphine, I was having to suction his throat.

Monday night, Broin and Frank went home and I fell asleep before I could set my alarm to give Tony his medicine. We all ironically slept peacefully.

I woke up Tuesday morning in a panic. I stared right at his chest. He was still breathing, but he hadn't moved all night. Tony was no longer responding.

Without saying anything to the boys, I got them up for school like every other morning. Around 9:30, Brooke and her aide gave him a bath, Broin gave him a shave, I sprayed him with smell good, Aqua D'Gio. My love was ready to go home. When I said I love you, he would slowly blink his eyes.

I knew he could hear me and was saying it back.

At 5:00 p.m. I called the boys and Tony's friends, and said time to come home. We hooked him up to a morphine drip. My love didn't deserve to suffer any longer. It was the hardest decision I ever had to make, but Tony was specific in his instructions and it was my responsibility to follow them.

I sat on the bathroom floor crying and asking for God's forgiveness. Selfishly I just wanted him here with me so we could still cuddle up at night. He had been sick for so long, it didn't seem any different. But it wasn't fair to him.

Around 9:23pm I called Brooke to ask her about his hands squeezing mine and Broin's hands. Frank then pointed out his breathing changed.

Nooo!

It's not happening.

I don't want him to go.

But there was nothing I could do. I had one hand on his chest and held his left hand while I lay next to him watching his chest go up and down with each breath.

There was no rattle. No gasping for air.

I just know that my hand was raising with each breath and then...my hand didn't move.

At that moment, I cried out in pain. My love, was gone. He left us and damn did it hurt. I didn't think about his pain being gone or suffering. I just wanted to wake up from the nightmare. My sister held me and everything at that point is a blur.

When I rolled over, Aydin had just woken up. "What's wrong mommy," he asked. Now I had to tell my ten year old that his Daddy had died. Aydin jumped up and saw Tony laying there and broke down.

"Daddy? Daddy!"

He wasn't sure if it was real. Aydin crawled into the bed with him and wouldn't let go. He didn't want to leave his daddy. I comforted him while my mom called Brooke and told her it was time to come. Just then I heard a loud bang. Alec punched the front door. His heart too shattered.

Brooke was amazing. She handled everything with tears pouring down her face. She's family now. She was broken hearted like all of us. Tony impacted her like he had done for so many others. She comforted me while ensuring my wishes were met when the funeral home arrived. Anthoney stayed with me while they came and took Tony.

I couldn't watch.

I couldn't watch him leave our home. Anthoney watched him all the way down the driveway.

That night, I slept with a pillow in my arms while Aydin slept in Tony's hospital bed. At 7:00 the next morning, Ashton came running downstairs and woke me up. "Mommy, where's daddy?"

My nightmare was real again.

"He's gone to heaven," I said. "He's with his family again." Ashton bursted into tears. "I didn't get to say good-bye mommy!" he cried. I reminded him that he did two days earlier when daddy told him that everything was going to be OK. He just laid in my arms and cried.

I knew then, it was our worst reality.

We all knew that this day would come. We all thought we prepared for it. But you can't *really* prepare for it. I would've done anything to have my love with me forever.

We were supposed to beat this together. Instead we experienced a deeper more beautiful love, and that I will hold on to forever.

But it hurts.

The pain is physical yet my heart is numb. I don't feel like answering the phone. I don't feel like going out. But the sun came up this morning. The alarm clocks went off. And I put the boys on the bus to school. It's going to take me time.

I'm never going to stop loving you Anthony Wayne Leonard.

I know you said I would be okay because I'm strong, but today, I'm not...and that my friends...is OK.

Forever His Legacy,
Forever My Love

How can I choose the right words to describe the *best* man in the world? He was the best father!! He was an amazing lover. And absolutely the *greatest partner* any one could ask for. He demanded hard work and dedication. He didn't believe in excuses. No matter how sick Tony was, he always showed up.

Especially for his boys. He was a father who lead by example, with strength. His battle was for his family, for the kids, for me. His boys made him proud. He couldn't be disappointed, if he wasn't proud. And to his boys...he was so proud so proud of you all. You are his legacy. You will carry on his name. Tony's legacy of strength, courage, and love for family is one that will continue to live on in every person he came into contact with.

He was a warrior and inspiration to so many. Tony made sacrifices for his family. He'd drive hours through the night just to make it to a birthday party while working on the road. He made it to sporting events despite his pain or sickness. He was the man that boys looked up to and strived to be. He believed you were whom you associated with, so associate yourself with winners.

Tony was a friend to all. But if you were a special friend, you were his family. Family was everything to Tony. He always said, "At the end of the day, family is all you have and can rely on." Especially, if your last name is Leonard. He'd always say to the boys, "You're a Leonard. It's in your blood, boy." But if Tony called you family, it wasn't about blood. It was about love and trust.

Tony proved to me that *true love* does exist. Tony loved me more than I loved myself. He loved my faults. He loved my freckles. He loved my smiles and my frowns. He knew how I was feeling by the look on my face, and he knew what kind of day I was going to have just by how I woke up.

Tony and I hated being apart. We could sit on the phone for hours and listen to each other breathe. If we blew up each others phones, it wasn't because we didn't trust one another, it was because we missed each other. Tony brought me roses when I was getting my hair done. It was our wedding anniversary. He was romantic and kind. I was his Queen and he was my King.

He exemplified how a husband treats a wife. He demonstrated passion and understanding. He trusted me with everything he had; and I him. He defended me and would always put me first. Sure, there were days that he'd drive me crazy, and I'd yell and fuss at him. But those moments would only last about five minutes.

Tony and I didn't sweat the small stuff. Because most likely it was all small stuff. Just thinking about him makes me smile, but it also makes me miss him oh so much.

I have no regrets. No stone was left unturned. We did everything we had ever wanted to do. No secrets. Nothing left unsaid. I am so blessed and grateful he allowed me to spend the rest of his life with him. And, for the rest of mine, I will love him forever.

What is the message?

Life is short, and it's what you make it. If you're happy, embrace it. If you're not, *do* something about it. Love one another and support your family and friends. Enjoy your life, because you only get one. Pick up the phone and call each other. Spend the day in bed with someone you love.

Tony always said, "Life is determined by the choices you make." Make the *best* of each moment and don't dwell on the bad. "Regardless of how bad the news is, you still have a tomorrow. The sun will still come up." (Tony Leonard) Life goes on. We're still going to get up every morning, and go to work, and school.

And no matter what, Tony is always going to be there. He's always going to be watching over us.

This journey has taught me what unconditional love is, but most importantly, it has taught me how to live.

CPSIA information can be obtained
at www.ICGtesting.com
Printed in the USA
LVHW020737201121
703853LV00001B/2